# MEMOIRS OF A HIGH FLYER

This book is dedicated to Keith Durbidge and his family and friends

# MEMOIRS OF A HIGH FLYER

## Keith Durbidge

**LULU.COM**

First published in Great Britain 2013 by Lulu
lulu.com

The right of Keith Durbidge to be identified as the author of this work has been asserted by him in accordance with the Copyright, Design and Patents Act, 1988.

Cover image © Imperial War Museum (E(MOS) 1325)

Copyright © 2013

ISBN: 978-1-291-30083-3

Printed and bound in Great Britain by lulu.com
Distributed by lulu.com

# Contents

List of Images

# Foreword

## By David Hart

Keith Durbidge was a man who was inspirational to everyone who met him and *"Memoirs of a High Flyer"* does the world of flying an extraordinary service by giving us a picture of that man. By offering us his memories from across his long life, he gives us a glimpse of his modesty and humour, his unassuming courage and of his skill as a pilot.

Here we see him as a family man and friend; as a dedicated and pragmatic leader who rose through the ranks to become a Squadron Leader in the R.A.F. and won the DFC and the DFM during some of the most dangerous years of World War II.

I first met Keith during the latter part of his flying career, when he was the Chief Flying Instructor at the Highland Flying Club based at Inverness in Scotland. At the time, I had no idea of his illustrious record, nor did he enlighten me. But, as time passed, and he taught me aerobatics, we became firm friends and I began to realise how fortunate we were. At times, upside down and hanging from the safety straps after a manoeuvre that had gone seriously wrong, his calm voice would come over the intercom, "My Dear Boy, I don't think we got that one quite right, shall we try it once again, please?" Always polite to a fault, his relaxed style would immediately put one at ease.

Slowly, always with a smile, he would remember some amusing incident from the war and we, who were too young to have been involved except as bystanders, would listen in rapt attention while he recalled it. In this man, one recognized a true professional; someone who knew the dangers waiting to trap the careless. He always instructed with a measured, sure, touch; he allowed his students to learn from their mistakes and was always quick to congratulate them when things went well. Above all, he was meticulous. There was no room for sloppy behaviour in the air. He loved flying and his love of flying was infectious.

His other love was for his family. Bunty, his wife, whom he adored, would invariably be around during Club functions and was always charming. The undoubted success of the Highland Aero Club, at that time as a

i

professional enterprise, has never been matched since his long tenure as CFI there. We were all devastated when he lost his licence for medical reasons but he continued to be associated with flying through the local R.A.F Association and the Keith Durbidge trophy which is presented each year to the winner of the spot landing competition.

Those who read this book will begin to realise the sacrifices made by those who fought and died during the war and of those wives and families who supported them.

I shall always be grateful to Keith for his sound advice and clear judgement. His influence in the Highlands was profound.

David Hart originally learned to fly in Sri Lanka where he was a tea planter. After retirement David moved back to England where he met Keith, "with such a wealth of experience, who was able to teach the finer points of aerobatics". After buying his own plane, aided by Keith, David flew for many years.

"There is absolutely no cure for the aviation bug – no cure at all!"

# Editor's Introduction

Keith Durbidge was a husband, father, grandfather, and Spitfire pilot. *Memoirs of a High Flyer* covers the life of Keith before, during, and after World War Two. Flying was a major part of his life alongside his family, and the stories told are mostly amusing insights into both of these important aspects.

Throughout this book you will find interesting stories from his travels, information on the war and different types of planes, however most importantly you will fall in love with Keith and the people around him.

From surviving the war, to sabotage attempts, to living around the world, Keith led an incredibly exciting life, and now it is time to share it with any reader who picks up this book.

Keith's story has touched my heart and made me smile. With the help of Lulu Publishers and Sheila Lambie we can now share his life with you. A special thank you also to David Hart for writing the Foreword and to James Ferguson at Signal Books for his continued support.

We hope you enjoy reading Keith's story.

Rebecca Rivers
Editor

The youngest picture we have of Keith. Here he is during flying training at Ponca City, Oklahoma, 1941.

# BEFORE THE WAR

# 1. A Sleepy Town

I WAS BORN at a very early age in Caversham, Oxfordshire, on 1st June 1921. This event was not the basis for naming the date, "The Glorious First of June", though some of my more generous acquaintances might argue otherwise on my behalf. The title was, in fact, given to one of Horatio Nelson's lesser-known victories over the French navy in the late 18th century. Apparently, British observers and spies became aware that a small French convoy of mainly treasure ships had left the West Indies bound for France and Napoleon's coffers. Nelson's spyships and warships had tracked this convoy and had destroyed it before it had reached safety in a French port. The final action had taken place on the first of June, 1797.

Caversham is a small town in Oxfordshire on the north bank of the River Thames opposite to, and overshadowed by Reading, the county town of Berkshire, famous for Huntley & Palmer's biscuits, Suttons Seeds, Symmonds beer and the Tin Box Manufacturers Ltd. Reading was also a University town, a major railway junction, the centre of a large agricultural community, and was fast becoming a dormitory town for London.

Although Caversham must have been a somewhat sleepy town, to me as a young schoolboy of seven or eight years it was vibrant in many ways. Caversham Motors, the main local garage, was located between my home and my school and it had six petrol pumps, two each of BP, Shell and National Benzole Mixture. These pumps were lined up along the footpath away from the road. There were few cars in those days, in fact I remember a period when I was a keen collector of car registration numbers

– most of them showed RG followed by four figures on the number plate, indicating that they were locally based – there were very few strangers! The petrol pumps were operated by hand by a garage employee who appeared every time a car stopped nearby. The driver remained in his seat whilst the employee collected the car keys and did the work. The pump was operated either by a wheel or a pump handle. A glass bowl measuring a gallon was mounted about ten feet above the ground and it fascinated me to watch the bowl fill up as the petrol was splashed into it. The operator would then leave the pump, make sure the hosepipe was securely inserted into the car tank and then release the fluid with a most satisfying gurgle for every gallon. The gurgle came from the petrol pipe, not the operator. While this was going on, a geared rod appeared from the top of the pump and rose up slowly as each gallon was fed to the pump's glass bowl. This rod, no doubt, was marked in such a way that fractions of a gallon could be delivered if required. It also triggered an indicator to the driver as to the total number of gallons so far supplied. This number remained on the indicator until the next car came along; this provided me with a simple game as I walked home from school, to guess the sequence of the numbers. Of course, if I had a friend with me we played marbles in the gutter instead and the petrol pumps were ignored. It was a hard day if it had been raining, and the gutters were awash, because the marbles wouldn't run well through the water. Only the big glass 'alleys', big as gobstoppers, were then of any use and there were very few boys who could afford them. (I wonder why they were called 'alleys'?)

In those days our favourite sweets were gobstoppers which changed colour as you licked away the layers; sugar mice with string for a tail and eyes made from 'hundreds and thousands'; sherbet fountains in flimsy triangular paper bags with a short, black liquorice pipe to suck up the sherbet; sherbet 'dabs', paper containers with a disc of toffee on a stick to reach the sugar at the bottom. If you had a lot of pocket money you could afford 'conversation lozenges' – sweet, scented, circular, rectangular or heart-shaped lozenges with printed messages on them such as 'Naughty Boy', 'Kiss Me', 'I Love You' or 'See You Tomorrow'. My favourites were the sugar mice but they were too costly. My weekly pocket money was sixpence but twopence of that was always reserved for my regular visit to the Caversham Electric Theatre on

4

Saturday afternoon to see a film show of a Wild West adventure starring Tom Mix or Roy Rogers, or perhaps a comedy with Laurel & Hardy or Buster Keaton or Harold Lloyd. There was also a serial on the programme to entice you back the next week.

I had a favourite uncle – at least he turned out to be my favourite uncle – who very rarely visited us, though he lived less than twenty miles away. On the one visit I remember he took my brother Eric and me aside and gave us each a half-crown coin, worth five weeks pocket money. He said, "Now go and spend it. Don't listen to your mother, she'll only tell you to put it in your moneybox. Spend it all on something you really want". I don't remember what Eric spent his on but I ran straight to the local sweet shop and bought thirty large sugar mice. Some I gave away but I know that I ate the majority. My mother was really angry. She said, "You'll be up all night and you'll be sick every ten minutes". My lovely uncle said, "No he won't. His craving for sugar mice reflects what his body needs. You don't put enough sugar in his diet". I agreed with him completely and I wasn't sick at all.

## 2. Gone Forever. Well... Until Tomorrow Anyway

I LIVED A SHORT DISTANCE from one of the two bridges which spanned the Thames and it was no problem to walk into Reading and marvel at the wonderful things to be seen. The Reading Fire Station with its gigantic, highly polished, red fire engines was a few hundred yards beyond the bridge. If the main fire station doors were open you could peep in and see the shiny steel pole down which the firemen would swoop from their upstairs restroom if the alarm sounded. I was never lucky enough to witness such an exodus, not even a practice one, but, many, many years later, I was privileged to be allowed to have a go myself at a high speed descent down that same pole – but that's another story. Strangely, at one time if a fire occurred in Caversham, the Reading Fire Brigade was not permitted to turn out because the responsibility for quenching the flames lay with the Oxfordshire Fire Service and the equipment had to come from Henley, seven miles away. Happily, things have changed since the Second World War.

Perhaps Caversham's real claim to fame lies in the establishment of one of the few radio listening stations in England. Housed in a secluded, guarded and high-walled area the Unit monitored radio signals from all over the world. I lived in Caversham for over twenty years and had no knowledge of the Station's existence. Its secret nature was well concealed and for all I know it is still there today.

I had a great affection in those days for trains. I still have.

There were only steam trains then of course. The noise; the bustle; the wonderful smell of steam, smoke and grease; the love that drivers, firemen, guards, and the public as well, had for the hissing, gleaming monsters which they knew would always reach their destination on time regardless of snow, ice or leaves on the line – are fond but distant memories. It was easy to sense the pride of a station master who would make damn sure that any train that stopped at his station would get away on time or he'd know the reason why. And, there were porters! They seemed a reasonably happy breed of men, always polite and helpful who would look after your belongings as if they were their own. They knew the train times, which platforms to go to and whereabouts to wait on that platform to get the best seats.

Whenever I could afford a penny for a platform ticket I would go to Reading station, pay my penny and climb up on the narrow metal bridge which spanned the three main railway lines. If I looked west, the line on my left carried trains from London Paddington which stopped for south and west destinations such as Weymouth, Torbay, the Cornish Riviera, Ilfracombe, and Bristol. The line also served express trains for south and north Wales, Oxford and The Midlands. The line on my right provided the last stopping place before London for all the fast trains from the north, west or south. It was the middle line that excited me most. Usually this 'through line' was reserved for non-stoppers such as lengthy goods trains forging their way steadily eastwards but if I could arrange to be at my favourite stance on the bridge at about 3:15 any afternoon I knew I was in for a short but thoroughly exhilarating experience. If I looked out to the west along the long straight middle line I would see a thin stream of white smoke in the distance. A faint whistle would be heard at 3:21 and then a continuous whistle, getting louder by the second, would start at 3:22. It was the Cheltenham Flyer, which would thunder through Reading station at exactly 3:23 each afternoon at 80 mph, next stop London, just a yard or so below me. The noise and speed; the smoke and steam; that piercing whistle; the tremendous vibration throughout the station – and through my bridge – a wonderful experience. A few seconds and he was gone – gone forever. Well… until tomorrow anyway.

Reading station was also a terminus for the green Southern Railway trains but you could sometimes see a long green passenger train struggle up the incline between the two station buildings on its way to the north and west using the Great Western track. Of course, boy-like, I preferred the chocolate and cream livery of the Great Western Railway.

8

# 3. Real Boys Didn't Play The Piano

ABOUT THAT TIME, 1927-1928, my parents made a momentous decision which required a great sacrifice from them. They decided that a Grammar School or Boarding School education for their sons was the best foundation for life they could give us. My father, a railwayman, always a railwayman, took up employment in Nigeria on railway work in order to improve the standard of life for his family. His salary from the Crown Agents for the Colonies was sufficient for their plan to be initiated. It meant of course that my mother stayed at home to provide for us boys and she didn't see my father for a tour period of eighteen months. He would then get eighteen weeks leave. He did two or three tours before my mother was able to join him. During his absences she developed a habit of writing long, long letters on thin foolscap paper. Eighteen or twenty pages every fortnight detailing everything that had happened at home. She had to work to a strict timetable because ships of the Elder Dempster Line sailed every second week on the West African route – no air mail in those days. Mother also kept a closely documented ledger of every expense incurred in running the home. She made sure that not a farthing was owing to anyone at the end of the month. A wonderful achievement. When she eventually managed to accompany Dad in Africa, Eric and I became the recipients of those long letters on thin paper, and how we looked forward to them!

I went to the Reading Blue Coat School (RBCS) as a 'day-boy' at the age of nine along with my brother Eric, who was two years my senior. At that time, there were about 48 boarders and approximately 60 day-boys at the school at Bath Road, Reading. In 1931 Eric and I became boarders, no longer having to walk the three miles to and from school every day. My mother would soon be able to go out to Nigeria to join Dad. During holidays, Eric and I went to friends in Coventry. When he left school Eric took up employment in that area with Courtaulds Ltd., and apart from his wartime service in the Royal Army Medical Corps he spent the rest of his life there.

The Reading branch of the Blue Coat Schools was founded in 1646 in the reign of Charles I, by Richard Aldworth who provided enough money to set up "basic education for eight God-fearing boys of good behaviour". His benevolent action was later supported by like-minded men and the School has survived. The benefactors' names were used to designate the small dormitories in Bath Road – Aldworth, Malthus, Rich, and West. Nowadays, in the 21st century, the RBCS is a thriving institution with plenty of money in the bank, excellent facilities for all aspects of modern education, and girls on the register. In my time, the School was a small organisation with big hopes and big problems. Five full-time staff were fully engaged in basic teaching and the Headmaster, Mr. W. F. W. King, known locally as 'The Mussolini of Bath Road' spent most of his time trying to keep the School's head above water. Mrs. King was matron, supervising a small female staff in the kitchen and treating minor ailments, cuts and bruises. Old Tom Pearson was a kind, long-suffering and very helpful gardener and handyman who, apart from his duties in producing as much as possible from the gardens, kept all the toilets clean and in good order.

Life as a boarder in the RBCS was certainly different from anything I had imagined. For a start we wore a uniform which mirrored the dress of the 17th Century schoolboy. Black shoes, yellow knee-length woollen stockings (not cross-gartered, thank heavens, as Shakespeare would have insisted), corduroy shorts with three silver buttons on the outer edge of each leg, a thick cotton shirt and a navy blue woollen jersey both worn throughout the year. For any special event like a Sunday church parade we wore a long black gown of barathea, I think, buttoned from waist to neck with silver crested buttons and fitted with a narrow leather belt around the waist. This ensemble was finished off with a six-inch long, well-starched, white cotton cravat which was attached to the collar of the gown. Woe betide you if you did not make that pristine cravat last two weeks. A boarder quickly learned to adopt the Navy's habit of 'Make do and Mend', so now, if necessary, I can darn my own socks, sew buttons on the stiffest of materials – the right way up – and repair short slits in essential garments. Laundry was changed weekly and major damage to shirts or pants was repaired by matron and her minions before the articles were returned, laundered. All garments were numbered; my number was 32, so you couldn't get away with any real damage to materials resulting from the usual rough-and-tumble activities that boys get up to. Explanations were required but abject apologies were generally accepted.

A boarder's day was fairly closely scheduled and controlled. We were routed from our beds by the duty Master at 0630 every morning; we threw back sheets and blankets to air them, filed down the stairs to the ablution area where we either showered (finishing off with a cold spray) or had a strip-down wash around one of the two circular 8-foot, deep green marble communal fountains. Back upstairs to get dressed and remake our beds. These tasks had to be completed by 7 o'clock. With no cleaning staff at the School, all the preparations and cleaning requirements for the day ahead were completed by the boarders and for this purpose we were divided into teams which were called 'Trades'. This division into Trades was made in September at the very beginning of the school year and remained unchanged, thus developing a healthy rivalry between the members of one team and the next.

The Dormitory team swept and dusted the three dormitories and swept the stairs to the ground floor. This was generally considered the softest option provided that you worked quietly (very difficult for ten to fifteen year olds) and didn't disturb the slumbers of the members of staff who also slept nearby.

The Schoolroom team, responsible for sweeping and cleaning the four classrooms, checking materials and equipment, worked quite hard before breakfast and lunchtime but was otherwise free.

The Lavatory or Ablutions team ensured that wash-hand basins, shower areas, bathrooms and surrounding corridors were thoroughly cleaned and polished. Taps always gleamed.

The most comfortably-off team, I always thought, was the Buttery mob. Their job was to sweep out the dining room ready for the three daily meals. Always in the warm and dry. No preparations, no washing up, just setting out the cutlery, mugs and plates. The kitchen staff did the cooking and food preparation. Only one drawback, they were still busy for the evening meal.

Finally the Utility Trade team, they had very little to do if it was raining except to sweep the covered pathways. If it wasn't raining they cleaned up the playground, which was a gravelled area almost as big as a football pitch. We were allowed an hour to complete the various tasks to the satisfaction of the Duty Master who inspected our efforts by 8 o'clock. Hands were washed and inspected and then we lined up for the daily ration of pure, raw yeast issued personally by the Headmaster who made sure you consumed the stuff by popping it into your mouth himself and by looking back as he moved down the line to make sure you hadn't disposed of it improperly. I eventually got to like it but many of my companions dreaded the ordeal. Someone had told the Headmaster that pure yeast cleared the blood and prevented boils and spots. None of his boys were going to get spots!

Into the buttery or dining hall by 8:15 for the regular breakfast fare. Slightly sweetened porridge all the year round with a choice, sometimes, in the summer term, of unsweetened cornflakes, a strongish mug of tea and as many thick slices of white bread and margarine as you felt you could eat. However many you chose, you had to eat them. Healthy but dull unless one of us had received a tuck box – then there might be Marmite or jam, or even marmalade on the table.

At half past eight we were free except for the Buttery crew who had to clear and clean the dining room, unless of course the Duty Master had not been happy with your own team's efforts. School started at 9 o'clock by which time all the day-boys had arrived. A short break at 11:00 allowed us to dash madly round the gravel playing ground. Lunch from 12:30 pm until 2:00 was another free period for some but the Buttery and Schoolroom crews would be busy. Lessons stopped at 4:30 and all the day-boys disappeared.

Wednesday afternoons were reserved for sports. We marched off to Prospect Park, a mile away, for soccer or cricket except for those boarders wicked enough to have been awarded detention for misdemeanours during the previous week. Detention was supervised by one of the Staff and always consisted of mental arithmetic exercises from a series of test manuals. My ability to carry out rapid (and accurate) mental calculations, especially in the modern supermarkets, has stood me in good stead.

Saturday afternoons were devoted to sport for all boarders, regardless of their desire to take part. A fairly well equipped gym was built alongside the playground for use when the weather precluded the march to Prospect Park. I didn't care for Sundays much. Two compulsory church parades, a morning service of Sung Eucharist and an evening visit for Evensong called for marches in full regalia two miles each way to and from St. Laurence's church near the market square in Reading. Sunday afternoons? Well, a compulsory letter home censored for spelling, punctuation and composition by the Duty Master and completion of any homework for the following week which had not been finished during the previous week's evening homework sessions.

Looking back on those days, I have come to realise how very fortunate I was. I learned to look after myself physically and personally and I developed a fair sense of responsibility, of respect for authority and superior knowledge. The school curriculum was comprehensive – English Literature, Grammar, Composition, Spelling, Handwriting (my worst subject, when I had completed a written article it looked almost indecipherable, rather like the average doctor's lengthy prescription and signature. We could only use pens with steel nibs and ink from inkwells, no biros then. Trouble was, my best friend who sat next to me produced perfect copperplate writing and he was left-handed and had to curl his left hand right round the pen so that he didn't smudge the paper). Other regular subjects were Arithmetic, Algebra, Geometry, Mental Maths, History, Geography, French, Commerce, Book-keeping (which I didn't like one bit), Pitman's Shorthand, Art, Practical Science, Woodwork, and if you chose to take it, Music. I have always regretted not taking Music, which at the time I considered was a cissy subject – real boys didn't play the piano. My end-of-term reports were generally very good because, I suppose, I enjoyed learning new things and I had already decided to become a teacher when I left school.

Keith in his flying gear ready to tackle the rigours of life at 30,000ft, 1944.

# DURING THE WAR

# 4. Scrumpy Blindness

BY THE TIME I was fifteen, in June 1936, both my parents were overseas and the Headmaster, Mr. King, took me on as a pupil teacher offering full board and lodging at the School with a princely offer of £2.00 per month pocket money. What a bargain he got! Three years later, when the Second World War started, fire-watching and emergency air-raid precautions were added to the duties of the teaching staff. I was still studying to get to university and passed the London Matriculation and the local University entry exams.

In September 1940 I entered Reading University to study for a Science degree. At that time I was living at home in Caversham, my mother having been obliged to return from Nigeria because of the war. All male students were required to join a military training system within the University, presumably to provide a modicum of training and experience should they fail their annual examinations and thus lose their 'reserved occupation' status. Reading University at that time just had the Army Cadet Corps facility which every student had to join. I hated Wednesday afternoons when we put on uniforms from the First World War and marched up and down the streets. I found the puttees to be the worst aspect of these activities – these cursed strips of greenish Hessian were wound round the legs and they regularly unravelled and threatened to trip you up. The only consolation was when a friend's puttee fell apart and you could, accidentally of course, tread firmly on it.

Thank Heavens, in early 1941 an Air Training Squadron was formed and we were allowed to transfer our allegiance. At least, on Wednesday afternoons the only 'square-bashing' we did was marching to a University lecture hall to be subjected to instruction on Navigation, Meteorology, Morse Code Signalling, Aircraft Recognition, Air Law, Airmanship, Aerodynamics, Principles of Flight, Hygiene and Sanitation, etc. This was no hardship; we were doing this sort of thing all day anyway.

At the end of the first year at the University these studies proved to be of great advantage to those of us who volunteered to join the R.A.F. for aircrew training. The standard we achieved in the regular tests we sat that year must have been high enough for all the volunteers to be accepted without having to undergo the irksome I.T.W. course (Initial Training Wing) which most RAF aircrew aspirants were required to complete.

My application to join up along with those of at least a dozen Reading University students was processed through the Air Training Corps at the University. Very shortly afterwards I received instructions to report to the Aircrew Reception Centre (A.C.R.C.) at St. John's Wood in London on a date which gave me two weeks grace. I had no money so I took up a night job for those two weeks at a large garage, Vincent's, just off the main square outside Reading Railway Station. This proved to be one of the many remarkable coincidences that I have experienced since that period. My nightly task was to issue, record, receive and repair sets of blueprints used by technicians who were constructing fuselage and tail units for Spitfire aircraft. The finished products were then painted a soft blue colour. Little did I know that within a year I would be flying these particular blue angels. I realise now that Vincent's garage was one of the many dispersed 'shadow factories' which proliferated during the war producing parts for aeroplanes, tanks etc. The intention was to spread production widely in order to reduce the chance of major losses during German air raids.

During that fortnight I was required to go to an Oxford address for a full medical and for Attestation – swearing allegiance to King and Country! It was a gloriously hot day and most of the work was completed before noon, leaving only ears, eyes, nose, and throat tests to be done. Lunch was simple – sandwiches, but a long drink was essential and we were lucky enough to find a small pub nearby which sold Scrumpy, a locally made cider. Two pints of that and a short snooze on the grass made a perfect solution to our requirements. However, there was a snag – there always is – and when we all arrived back at the Test Centre the eye test proved to be impossible. In my case, when asked to read off the letters on the wall chart I couldn't even see the chart. We got away with it however, because all my colleagues were in the same boat. Our humble explanations were accepted, no doubt this was not the first time the medical staff had encountered communal Scrumpy blindness on a very hot day.

We all reported to the A.C.R.C. on the big day and underwent numerous strange experiences. There were hundreds of young men there, all being processed for differing schemes of aircrew training in different parts of the world. Only the authorities knew who was where, when and how. What a perfect opportunity for chaos to reign – but it didn't. The only snag that I encountered was that my surname was incorrectly spelled on all the documents I ever saw. I tried for a long time to get the Personnel Department to delete the second 'r' but I eventually gave up – what's in a name, anyway?

Our contingent was housed at Abbey Lodge, fed at Lord's Cricket Ground and marched up and down and round about whenever there was nothing else to do. One day we were fitted out with grey suits with matching accessories, (which gave rise to much ribald speculation) but a few days later these were taken back and we received proper R.A.F. uniforms and equipment for our exalted rank of Aircraftmen Second Class (A.C. 2). We were vaccinated or inoculated for pretty well every disease known to man except perhaps tennis elbow or housemaid's knee. One day our group from Reading University was taken to an unknown destination and tested in a decompression chamber. The aim of this exercise was, I believe, to impress on us the need for oxygen to be used on all flights at the upper altitudes or at night. I was one of three guinea pigs chosen to demonstrate what happens if a lack of oxygen develops during a climb to height. The other five trainees looked on. We three were given a pad of paper and a small pencil and were told just to write down our names and addresses until told to stop. Everyone was fitted with an oxygen mask but only the five 'observers' masks were turned on. I clearly remember thinking that this was a doddle, in fact I even settled down to try to produce some copybook handwriting. I kept on writing, convinced that with every moment that passed my signature was improving and that I could keep this up at any height. Shortly afterwards the operator switched the oxygen on again and told us to examine our notepads.

Mine was a mess. After the first few signatures my writing began to wobble and finally it became an indecipherable scribble ending in a pencil line trailing off into nothing. And I had been so pleased with myself and my handsome script. For me it was a telling demonstration. I was careful to ensure during my operational career that my oxygen system was serviceable before take-off and remained so throughout the flight.

Our time at the A.C.R.C. was short. To my knowledge, we were never told what our fate was going to be and I don't remember our discussions or speculations being seriously followed through. Things happened very swiftly. One morning we were instructed to get all our gear together. Big canvas kitbags with our names and numbers already printed on them were issued and, still unaware as to our destination, we were hustled into buses and taken to Kings Cross Station. No time to send a note to parents or families. No indication on the train where it was going and the train staff, "Did not know, sorry". The only excitement was when a motor cycle and sidecar raced onto the platform and the driver shouted "A.C. 2 Johnson". Johnny was the shortest of all our Reading Uni members. They disappeared in a cloud of dust and exhaust fumes. By now tongues were wagging and we wondered what Johnny had done to deserve being abducted. An hour later, with the train still waiting, and our speculations getting more outrageous every minute Johnny re-appeared by the same means and re-joined us. He said, "I was taken to an R.A.F. Station, possibly North Weald, told to put on a parachute and stuffed into the cockpit of a Hurricane. Some technician moved the seat to and fro to see if I could reach the controls. It seems that I'm big enough, just, so I was brought back here. What a hairy ride that was through London traffic. The driver couldn't tell me what it was all about – maybe he didn't know either".

When the train eventually moved off, we were no further forward as to our guesses on what was happening. It was dark when the troop-train stopped after a very lengthy journey. Few of us were any wiser when we read the name of the Station, Gourock. No doubt that something serious was going on because the next thing we did was to board an immense ship, the French liner 'Louis Pasteur', a former winner of the 'Blue Riband of The Atlantic'. This vessel was so fast that it made many journeys across the North Atlantic without naval escort. Our trip was one of those. We did have one scare two days out when the look-out signalled an alarm but with a swift change of course nothing else happened.

That first night on board was disastrous for me. We airmen were fitted with greatcoats and allotted various locations on board, which had to be patrolled or guarded. We were given a rifle (which was a new device to me – I hardly knew which end to be scared of) but no ammunition and told not to allow anyone, but ANYONE, to pass the door we were guarding. The Louis Pasteur was still in harbour but there was a slight, uneasy swell and a faint but definite rolling motion. My particular location was the Officers' Dining Room and their meal was about to be served. Soon after taking up my post I began to feel queasy. Seasickness, like airsickness, cannot be disregarded once it has taken over command in the stomach. Life is not worth living for the sufferer. All other considerations fade away – one just wishes to die and as soon as possible, please. After a period of rapid swallowing I knew that I was going to be sick. I propped my useless rifle against the door I was supposed to be guarding with my life, staggered to the ship's rail and deposited the contents of my bewildered stomach into the River Clyde. This did not relieve the situation nor did it allow me to regain a desire to live. How long it took me to become human again I do not know. In fact, I have no idea what occurred during the next ten or twelve hours. All I can recall now, after more than 60 years, is that a notice was posted on the board and in Standing Orders to the effect that, "No-one on guard duty may relinquish his post at any time or for any reason on pain of court martial". I heard no more of that unpleasant episode but I was not put on guard duty again. I wonder why?

We arrived in Halifax, Nova Scotia, five days later after what was, to me, a fine four days holiday. My recovery from that first night's horror was rapid – after all, at 20 years of age one's physical system does not suffer for long. From Halifax to the Royal Canadian Air Force Station at Moncton, New Brunswick, by rail took little time but we still had no idea of our final destination. Moncton was being used as the main base for Air Force personnel in their hundreds who were being sent for training in various Canadian and American Units. It was also the final assembly point for trained aircrews returning to the U.K.

No wonder RCAF Moncton was being enlarged at a furious rate. Wooden buildings springing up everywhere, deep ditches all over the place to take water and sewage pipes to and from those buildings (Canadian winters can be early and very severe and they needed to be buried very well down). Moncton earth is a pretty pink clay, and guess who slipped whilst crossing an icy wooden plank over a 6ft ditch half filled with icy pink water? And guess who had to let go of his kitbag in order to keep his balance? My letters home for months were a source of amusement to my colleagues – and to my mother. No parades or inspections were called for or I might have been put on a fizzer for having shirts, collars and uniform of an unauthorised colour.

At last we were told our destinations. Thirty of us, including the Reading University contingent were destined for a town called Ponca City in Oklahoma. We were to join No. 6 British Flying Training School (BFTS) where the instructors were American civilians and the airfield was also civilian-run. Our first reaction to the news was delight. We could tell our families where we were and where we were going. It was just as well that I wrote to my mother in Caversham because about four weeks after we had left for the London A.C.R.C., there was a knock on the door and when Mother answered it the local policeman, a very friendly, fatherly chap said, "I am terribly sorry to have to approach you in this matter but I have to obey orders. I have a colleague with me and we have come to apprehend your son Keith. The rear entrance to the garden is covered and the best thing for all would be for your son to give himself up and come with me. I've known you and your family for many, many years and I am truly sorry to have to do this. I am instructed to arrest him on a charge of being a deserter. I am so very sorry". My mother had an impish sense of humour and could not resist saying, "But he's not here. Not here at all. He hasn't been here for weeks. Call your officer friend in for a cup of tea. It must be thirsty work waiting to catch a criminal". The unhappy constable said he could not possibly do that; he had his duty to perform. I think mother quite enjoyed the first minute or so of teasing him but then relented and said, "I had a letter from Keith about ten days ago, you'd better read it". She fetched the letter. The bobby read it and said, "Thank you for that – I knew your Keith and I couldn't believe the charge.

You've had me on a string this morning – we'll have that cup of tea now please, and wish him luck from me next time you write".

# 5. A Spark Of Ability

OUR PARTY LEFT MONCTON by rail and travelled directly to Chicago. There we boarded a train, which to me brought back memories of American films and songs from pre-war times. 'The Atchison, Topeka and the Santa-Fe' turned out to be a real train, running from Chicago to Mexico's border and, by chance, stopped at Ponca City, Oklahoma. It was boiling hot in the carriage reserved for us and getting hotter by the minute so we naturally opened all the windows. By doing so we incurred the displeasure of the Conductor who swept into our carriage and closed them all again. He said, "This train is fitted with the latest air conditioning system and the windows must stay closed for it to work. It will be quite cool in about twenty minutes". And it was! During that journey to Ponca City our coach was frequently 'invaded' by all kinds of Americans keen to see what these British boys were like. At every stop we were offered food, drinks and goodies by groups of well-wishers who were waiting for the train to arrive. Somehow they knew we would be in R.A.F uniform instead of those grey suits.

I was fascinated by the gloomy hooting by the train driver every time we approached a road-rail crossing – just like the mournful sound on the Hollywood movies when Roy Rogers just managed to jump over the line and escape the pursuing 'baddies'. Ponca City at first sight seemed to me to be the epitome of Hollywood's small American country town with its drugstore, (Cuzalina's in this case) and having the railway track dividing the town into the haves and have-nots. Life was so very different for our party. Excellent food in abundance. No rationing, no blackout, no restrictions on movement, no shortages, no queuing. Plenty of everything you could afford to buy. Not that this bounty was available to us really, with our low pay packets and the intensive training programme. We started immediately on our flying course at the 'Darr School of Aeronautics' at the airport a couple of miles outside Ponca City.

The whole Course of training up to R.A.F. 'Wings' standard was divided into three Sections: PRIMARY in which we flew the famous Stearman biplane, the type that you can still see at Airshows flying smoothly with a pretty girl walking the wing. I cannot recall ever having one walking my wing, I'm sure I would have noticed. The Stearman was like a very sturdy Tiger Moth, the British equivalent, with a cruising speed of 90 mph. The BASIC Section was represented by the Vultee Valiant, a monoplane, much heavier and more powerful than the Stearman and which cruised at a little over 100 mph. The third Section: ADVANCED, required the trainee to make quite a leap forward with the Harvard. This aircraft was considerably more powerful. It required much more delicate handling especially in landing manoeuvres. It was more sophisticated in presentation of information to the pilot and it introduced the trainee to such marvels as the variable pitch propeller. It produced the loudest and most annoying noise to the man on the ground especially when the propeller pitch was changed or the aircraft passed by. I remember when, much later, I was flying Harvards on instructional work for the Royal Navy in North East England, as we were behind schedule we had to fly on New Year's Eve. I deliberately flew over the house in Newcastle, operated the engine throttle and pitch control at midnight knowing that it would remind my wife that she had a husband after all.

My first flight at Ponca City took place on November 3rd 1941. Shortly after that I was almost in despair because however much I tried to control my diet I was physically sick on almost every flight I made, and this meant that little or no learning progress was being made. This was a bleak forecast for any pilot trainee in those days who was unable to make the necessary progress. He would be sent to Canada to retrain as a Navigator or Observer. A terrible fate.

Fortunately for me my instructor, Mr. Myers, must have seen a spark of ability somewhere and he enlisted the support of the base doctor. After 9 hours of flying I was sent aloft for a suspension flight with Mr. Anderston who was, I think, of benevolent disposition that day, because he recommended a further period of training. The support of my own instructor, and the doctor, and Mr. Anderston's recommendation gave me the chance I needed to continue pilot training. My tendency towards airsickness slowly receded and after about twenty hours flying I had caught up with my colleagues on No. 3 Course. Three weeks after my first flight I went solo on the Stearman and we completed the Primary stage of the Course by mid-January 1942.

Normally Oklahoma did not experience very cold winters but 1941-1942 changed all that. We had a fine time snowballing in between flights and I believe Ponca citizens were regularly calling up the local Radio Station (I still remember its call sign KBJA) saying things like "Hello there, Mrs Thornton J. Wilson of 27 East Third Street has seen snowflakes falling in her garden. No fooling, real white snowflakes". That year, Ponca had snowfalls to the depth of 4-5 inches and the Poncans eventually gave up reporting and boasting about the amount of snow experienced.

The Basic part of the Course on the BT13 (Vultee Valiant) took us to mid-March during which we spent a considerable amount of time on cross-country, formation, and night and instrument exercises. Finally, on to the Advanced trainer, the AT6 Harvard. All exercises carried out previously were covered in the Advanced stage of the Course. My last flight took place on May 1st 1942 by which time I had completed 187 hours flying dual and solo, day and night.

We kicked our heels awaiting movement orders for nearly a month. One happy event was the presentation of our 'Wings', the prize we had all been striving for, by a visiting R.A.F. Officer, and our sudden elevation to the dizzy rank of Sergeant. It was, to me, a mountain climbed, to be able to say I was a sergeant pilot, Royal Air Force.

In those days, Ponca City (home of the Ponca Indians) was the headquarters of the Continental Oil Company (Conoco) and the great majority of local folk were directly or indirectly employed in the oil business. On our arrival in 1941 my friend Geoff Lewis and I were able, on the first

Sunday to visit Ponca and gaze wide-eyed at its delights after the horrors of life in Europe. Everything we used to know and enjoy was there – and much more. We were stopped in the main street that day by an American couple, a Mr. & Mrs. MacDowell Gray, who invited us to their house for lunch. Naturally we thanked them and said we'd be delighted to have a chance to forget the war for a while – we had not been paid yet anyway and lunch was going to be a sandwich and a coke in the drugstore. Mr. Gray was a senior staff member of Conoco. These two kind and charming Americans made it a feature of the next six months to look after the two of us every Sunday if we were free. Their two young children were equally charming and Geoff and I always looked forward to our Sundays off. This American generosity was characteristic of the people throughout – I believe all the British and 'allied' young men received the same kindness and consideration all over the States. Basically, the average American was firmly anti-Nazi and was keen to do his or her bit to 'help the cause'.

Geoff and I were lunching with the Grays on the Sunday when the Japanese bombed Pearl Harbour and the announcement was made when we were at lunch. Mr. Gray said, "Ah, now we are officially on your side. It's what I have been hoping for". I believe Geoff said something like, "We are very glad to have you with us". If he had been an American, Geoff would very likely have added "Surr".

At last, after a seemingly endless struggle, we were back at Moncton in Canada but this time we were heading in the opposite direction, back to the war. In no time at all we were out at sea, this time on the 'Duchess of York'. This ship was another high-speeder but instead of forging her way through the Atlantic she rolled along. No wonder she was known as 'The Drunken Duchess'. I considered myself very unfortunate indeed because I celebrated my 21st Birthday on board, and the Duchess was dry, not even a watery beer could be obtained!

# 6. The Port Wing Stayed In The Tree

OUR RETURN TO EUROPE gave us a very clear example of the difference between the two 'worlds' that fringed the North Atlantic – or perhaps the Authorities wanted to make sure that we wanderers knew that we were back to the fight because when we disembarked at Liverpool and boarded a train for Bournemouth our first meal consisted of 'Ship's Biscuits', a four inch square by one inch thick rock hard biscuit, honey-combed with tiny holes and, I'm sure, made from flour, cement, and hard water. I suppose the many weevils that appeared when the biscuits were tapped were intended as protein for the troops. A happy introduction back to 'Dear ol' Blighty'.

After a few days in Bournemouth a dozen or so of us were sent up to Tern Hill, an R.A.F. Station in Shropshire, where pilots who had been trained abroad were converted to British systems, wartime techniques and procedures (e.g. the phonetic alphabet, A for 'orses, B for mutton, C for yourself etc.). Tern Hill was equipped with Master Aircraft. The Mark I used the Rolls-Royce Kestrel engine and was slightly lighter on the controls than the Mark III which had the radial Twin Wasp engine. The Mark II Master, also radial, was fitted with the Mercury XX engine.

Our contingent of trainees arrived at Tern Hill on a cloudy, wet Saturday evening and we immediately retired to the Sergeants' Mess bar where I managed to locate my instructor-to-be, F/Sgt Johnson. Over a friendly beer he gave me a general picture of the ground we had to cover. He said that the next day, a Sunday, was forecast to have low cloud, rain and poor visibility all day. However, if I would like to get airborne, try out the Master and get a look at the local countryside, etc. he would arrange it. I readily agreed. At last, flying an RAF aircraft and on the first real step towards operational work. This 'first step' turned out to be a stumble. We took off at about 10:00 a.m., spent most of the next forty minutes on handling exercises. We turned for home and passed over Nantwich, in Cheshire, at about 300ft. above the ground where some boys were playing cricket. They waved to us, we waggled the wings in reply and the engine stopped.

My instructor in the rear seat said, "What the hell have you done? What did you switch off? What did you touch?" I denied having touched anything. We turned away from the town, passed over a road, a railway and a canal and headed towards some fields half a mile away. At about 50ft. up I could see from the front cockpit that although we would miss the hedge we could not hope to avoid a tree directly ahead. Johnny in the back seat could not see the tree so I pressed hard on the right rudder and slewed the aircraft enough to hit the tree with the port wing instead of the engine. The impact swung us hard to the left and the port wing stayed in the tree. The aircraft hit the ground sideways, the propeller went bowling across the field like an athlete doing cartwheels, and the tail section broke off to the right. We juddered to a stop in the middle of the field with the starboard wing still attached to the fuselage. The engine had concertinaed in to the front cockpit but the only injury to me was a cut on the knee and a pint or two of hot oil over my flying suit.

We abandoned what was left of our aeroplane and Johnny stated that the Regulations required one of us to guard the aircraft while the other went for help. He said he had noticed a farmhouse beyond the field so he would go up there to phone Tern Hill while I was to stand guard. I asked him which bit he would like me to guard and he decided that the cockpit, engine and fuselage would be more suitable than the other bits which were too widely scattered. He disappeared over the hill and about an hour later I saw him staggering back towards me. He told me in a somewhat slurred voice that I was to go and clean up at the farm beyond the hill and that the Engineering people from Tern Hill were on their way.

As I reached the farmhouse the farmer's wife invited me in and suggested that I should have a good wash to get rid of the oil. There was a deep sink filled with hot water all ready for me and as I was washing myself a large tumbler of neat whisky appeared at my elbow. I was advised not to leave any since I had had a severe shock and whisky was the best cure. Subsequently I had a delightful tea with strawberries and real farmhouse cream, a delicacy I'd not had for years. When I eventually got back to the crash scene a WAAF driver in a Hillman van was helping to load our parachutes into the van. I recall that on our way back to Tern Hill we encountered another Hillman van, this one driven by the Engineering Officer coming to examine the aircraft. It seemed that he had rounded the corner on this winding Shropshire road and had immediately come across a young boy doing tight turns on his cycle in the middle of the road. In order to avoid hitting the boy he had driven through the hedge into a ploughed field and couldn't get out because he'd damaged the steering mechanism. Our WAAF driver promised to have another vehicle sent out to rescue him but she had strict instructions to return at once. Johnny and I got the distinct impression that she was secretly delighted at his predicament and would have a good story to relate to the other drivers.

I included this episode in a discussion we had, 36 years later, when I was running the Highland Aero Club at Dalcross Airport near Inverness. One Member, Geoff Farr, said he lived at Crewe in Cheshire and would like to delve into this incident; he later wrote to say, and I quote, – "From the clues you gave me and some local research I did, I am now able to tell you with some certainty that the crash landing took place at Marsh Farm, Marsh Lane, Nantwich. I have visited the site of the landing and had it confirmed from two sources. The first came from James Knowles, a long-standing friend, who remembered seeing the aircraft from a passing train soon after it crashed. This was confirmed by Larry Hankey who lived at Marsh Farm and was in his late teens at the time. The lady who treated you so well was his mother who kept house for the farm owner, alas both now dead. An odd thing, reflecting the wartime attitude to keeping secrets – an old lady who had lived in a farmhouse four or five hundred yards from the crash site said she had never been told about it, and it was the first time she was aware it had happened".

29

The authorities immediately assumed that the accident was due to some action or carelessness on my part as an ignorant trainee. (It is always aircrew error where doubt exists.) However, two days later, I was exonerated because a policeman had reported that he had been on point duty in the centre of Nantwich, had seen the aircraft fly overhead and had noticed that something had seemed to fall from it. A young boy had picked it up and had tried to run home with it. The policeman had seized the object and had been instructed to take it to the nearest R.A.F. Station. It turned out to be the carburettor air intake located beneath the cowling of the engine. No air intake – no air to the carburettor – no engine! I was not impressed by my first U.K. flight. Another strong coincidence, the boy and the policeman working on my behalf!

Two weeks later we were all thrilled to get our hands on a Front-Line Fighter. Each member of our group got airborne in a Hawker Hurricane, a wonderfully exhilarating experience compared with the Harvard and the Master. On looking back, I wonder if the Powers That Be deliberately provided the Hurricane for a "dabble" at this powerful aircraft. A few days later we thirteen newly qualified pilots were given the choice for our operational futures between three possible postings – Tank-Busting Hurricanes, Army co-operation in Lysanders, or P.R. We all wanted to be fighter pilots of course, preferably in Spitfires, nobody wanted Army co-op and we didn't know what P.R. was, so we all opted for the Hurricanes.

We were sent up to R.A.F. Hawarden, near Chester, for selection by the Flying Wing Adjutant. One by one the course pilots were approved and I happened to be the last to be interviewed because I had been talking to the Orderly Room staff. When I entered the Adjutant's office he looked up and said, "Who are you?" I explained and he said, "I've got the twelve pilots I need. You go back to Tern Hill for your next posting".

The next day I reported to the Tern Hill Adjutant who asked me what the hell I was doing back there. I explained what had happened at Hawarden. He looked up my record to see what I had given as my second choice of posting. He said P.R. was available so he was sending me to R.A.F. Fraserburgh to No. 8 (Coastal) Operational Training Unit (OTU). I asked him what P.R. was and was told, "Oh, I think it's Photographic Reconnaissance. You'll be flying Spitfires". So, in the end I got what I wanted. Little did I know that P.R. proved to be the most satisfying and rewarding of wartime occupations that I could have chosen.

# 7. Meeting The Spitfire

ON THE NEXT DAY, en route for R.A.F. Fraserburgh where No. 8 (Coastal) OTU was located, I entered Scotland for the first time in my life. I was fascinated by the countryside, by Edinburgh, the Forth Bridge and the grey granite city of Aberdeen. However, travelling further north to Fraserburgh I was completely bemused by the conversations by the folk in the compartment with me. I didn't understand a word. It took me quite a time before I could decipher the language of north-east Scotland, especially the Buchan tongue.

In those days there was a single-track spur of the railway from Fraserburgh to the three small fishing villages of Cairnbulg, Inverallochy and St. Combs. The little engine which pushed or pulled its way along, depending on whether it was going to or coming from, seemed permanently attached to the two passenger coaches, the single goods wagon, and the guard's van. The train had a smooth level run for about three miles parallel to the road and then faced a fairly stiff climb up on to the hill where the aerodrome was located. There was a halt at the bottom of the hill near where the WAAF quarters and equipment stores were and if passengers or goods had to be unloaded an additional ten minutes had to be added to the journey for the train to backtrack a mile or so to get up enough speed to tackle the incline. It is the only railway system that I have known that provided a hitch-hiking facility for the public because we were walking to The Broch, as Fraserburgh was called, of an evening for a pint or two. The train would trundle down the hill and along the flat, toot its whistle if the driver saw us and stop to allow us to cross the twenty yards of ground to climb aboard. It cost us twopence to get to The Broch. On one occasion when a fair number of us took the train back to Base from The Broch we all had to get out half way up the hill when it puffed to a stop. We walked to the top while the train retreated a mile or more to get up speed to reach the crest where we climbed aboard again for the rest of the journey.

I'll never forget Fraserburgh because it was there I met the Spitfire. Flying it was like strapping a pair of angel wings to your back. I also met Christine who tried hard to teach me the rudiments of Scottish Country Dancing. She had a friend who worked in the Station Orderly Room where I was posted for my first operational tour. She knew four days before we officially did that I was destined for No.69 Squadron in Malta, in company with two of my close colleagues, Sgt. Bob Leupke, an American, and Sgt. Trevor Howard, a Kentish man – or a man of Kent – I never remember which is which.

Training at Fraserburgh was intensive. Solo on the Spitfire followed by general handling exercises and local area reconnaissance prepared us for the main task of the O.C.U. There were twelve pilots on our course, and most of our Ground Training consisted of low and high level pilot navigation techniques, theory of oblique and vertical camera coverage, and the use that can be made of meteorological conditions to help a pilot complete his mission. It was drummed into us that... "The P.R. pilot's task depended for success solely on his own personal ability to plan his flight accurately, to carry out the navigation, to close limits to and from the targets, cover them adequately and return to base with the essential photographs and a visual report. You'll be on your own and unescorted and you'll be unarmed. Once the briefing is over you are your own boss and you are the only person who can decide exactly how you go about the task. Your main advantages over the enemy are threefold: (i) Your aircraft is carefully camouflaged, highly polished and has no guns or cannon to upset the smooth airflow over the wings, (ii) you have about three times as much fuel on board as any other single-engine aeroplane which means that if you are jumped you can turn away and run (if you see him first) until he gets short of fuel and gives up, then you can return and continue the task, and (iii) the Germans are getting short of fuel and unless they have a patrol already in your area and about your height they may consider it not worth their while to intercept. They know very well from their radar and from past experience who you are and what you're doing there. They don't know your targets though and they may just hope your route will take you somewhere close to their anti-aircraft batteries."

On the flying side at the O.C.U. we concentrated on low-level navigation, mainly over the sea (e.g. Base, direct to Sumburgh in the Shetlands, to the Butt of Lewis and back), with oblique photos of turning points; high level navigation with vertical photos of selected targets (e.g. York, Bristol, Manchester Airport and Carlisle); and bad weather flying practice (dual in the Master aircraft and solo in, of course, the Spitfire). We were much shaken when our numbers were reduced to eleven – the New Zealand member of the course lost control of his Spitfire in high-level cloud and spun into the ground close to Montrose airfield before he could recover.

After training had been completed three of us who were destined for Malta left Fraserburgh for R.A.F. Benson in Oxfordshire in early October 1942 to collect three new Spitfires.

# 8. Somebody's Iddon Him

WHEN I LEFT the U.K. for Malta to begin my first operational tour I should have been accompanied by two colleagues, one was Sgt. Bob Leupke, an American who had joined the R.A.F. before the U.S. entered the war and who frequently asked the operations staff at Benson to allow him to do at least one flight over enemy territory to gain the necessary experience before he left for the Mediterranean. He was given permission to fly to two targets near the Channel coast of France. He was shot down by German fighters shortly after arrival over France and did not survive the attack.

Trevor Howard and I flew down to R.A.F Portreath in Cornwall in brand new Mark IV Spitfires and after a day's delay due to bad weather took off separately for Gibraltar.

The airfield at Gibraltar was completely stacked out with aircrafts of all shapes, sizes and types, thus leaving a narrow corridor in which to land. The reason for this became apparent the next morning when we flew direct to Malta. It was November 7th and the start of the Allied attack on German and pro-Axis forces in North-West Africa. Scenes of fighting were clearly visible along the coasts of Morocco, Algeria and Tunisia, including the Royal Navy's attack on the French Navy at Oran.

A few weeks after joining No. 69 Squadron at R.A.F. Luqa, Malta I was hospitalised, as Bob Leupke would have said, with an ear infection which stopped me flying. While I was away from the Squadron, Trevor Howard was shot down returning form a sortie.

He bailed out over the sea a few miles from Malta and managed to get into his dinghy but was shot up and killed by his attacker.

My Squadron Commander on No. 69 Squadron was Wing Commander Adrian Warburton, a very highly decorated pilot and a very fine C.O. He had a great sense of humour and was thoroughly respected by pilots and ground crews alike. A book entitled 'Warburton's War' by Tony Spooner gives a good account of Warby's exploits in the Mediterranean theatre of war. Many true stories are told of his courage and perseverance as a reconnaissance pilot in low-level Baltimores and Marylands as well as in high-level Spitfires. He is the only pilot I have heard of who was fired at by anti-aircraft guns from above!

This came about well before the invasion of Sicily when the Task Force planners and military commanders were making early plans for an eventual assault on the so-called 'soft underbelly of Europe'. The island of Pantellaria, which had a fighter airfield located on it and which lies between the northern coast of Tunisia and the western end of Sicily, sits like a mattress on the sea. With cliffs up to 400ft. around most of the island there are few places where an attack would be feasible. Warby's task was to photograph the whole coastline using an oblique camera. He completed the work in one sortie. In the event, Pantellaria gave up before any attack could be mounted. An interesting feature concerning the surrender – the fighter airfield on the island was a large grass expanse eminently suitable for its task and an immense hangar built deeply into a hill at one side. The hangar was fitted with heavy electric doors, which provided ideal and safe housing for all the aircraft. It was also an ideal refuge for the islanders who ran there for shelter when the air raid sirens sounded. They felt the island was impregnable as long as the hangar doors would close in good time. However, just before the invasion of Sicily began, a lone Allied fighter-bomber bounced a 500lb bomb into the hangar and jammed the doors before they could be closed. Shortly afterwards the island surrendered.

The principal task for No. 69 Squadron was to provide regular visual and photographic coverage of the enemy's land, sea and air forces; their strengths; their movements; and their lines of communication. A close eye was kept on a regular basis for any ship heading to or from the North African coast where the German and Italian armies, under Field Marshal Rommel, opposed Montgomery's 8th army in the East. Later the Allied forces invaded Africa from the West.

Whenever an Allied convoy to Malta was planned or was in passage from Alexandria or Gibraltar, the Squadron was required to obtain, regardless of weather conditions, coverage of the three main Italian naval bases of Taranto, Naples and Messina where at least five battleships and twelve cruisers were stationed. Each day, three sorties were flown, one at first photographic light, one at noon, and a final one at last light, to ensure a convoy's safety, at least from large surface craft. Pilots on these particular sorties were authorised to disregard the instructions to maintain radio silence. They were to report 'in the clear' and, of course, in code, any capital ship that was absent from its usual moorings. On this information, whole convoys could be ordered to turn back.

Other demands on the Squadron might be made by military authorities from time to time and if it was not feasible to satisfy such a requirement within the regular scheduled tasks, additional flights would be made. One such request was given to me, I recall, just after the successful invasion of Sicily. I was to fly to Francesca in Sicily where a new airstrip had been cut out of a huge field of melons and grapes. My brief was to land there in the evening and do whatever the local Army Commanders wanted the next day. My memory of the tasks requested is quite blank but I do remember vividly my sheer delight the next morning when I stretched my arm out of the pup tent and found I had a choice of delicious melons and grapes within reach. After Malta rations this was heaven.

When I first joined 69 Squadron it was divided into two Flights, one for high level reconnaissance and the other for low level reconnaissance. The two Flight offices were next to one another and shared a telephone that stood in a hatchway between them. One day the phone rang and, being the nearest, I picked it up. A voice said, "I want to speak to Pilot Officer Iddon, the Engineering Officer". I said, "He iddon here" and put the phone down. A minute or so later it rang again and a member of the other Flight picked it up. We heard him say, "Sorry, somebody's iddon him". A third time the phone rang and another member of the Flight said, "No, sorry, he's not here, iddon it a shame". Shortly afterwards the bell rang again and that voice said, "I am Sir Keith Park. I am the Air Officer Commanding. I would very much like to speak to Pilot Officer Iddon. Do you think that could be arranged?" A pause, "Yes, Sir, we'll get him for you at once".

# 9. Sabotage Attempt

DUE NO DOUBT to the increased workload as the war in the Mediterranean area hotted up, No. 69 Squadron was reformed in early 1943. The low level Flight of Baltimores and Marylands was retained as No. 69 and the high level Spitfires were reformed as No. 683 Sqn. With Wing Commander Warburton in Command.

One morning, Warby called me in and said, "Keith, have you ever thought about taking a Commission?" I said, "No sir, I've been too busy being a sergeant pilot". He said, "Well, think about it". About twenty minutes later he said, "Well, have you thought about it? Because you have an interview with the A.O.C this afternoon at 2 o'clock". Sometime later I received notification of my Commission and Warby was the first to congratulate me. He also had a set of P/O stripes in his pocket to give me. "Sew these on now and report to the Officers' Mess at noon." I did as I was told and he bought me my first drink in the Mess. Ten minutes later he said, "Keith, you've been drinking; I'll take your flight this afternoon". And he did! The rogue. This was typical of Warby. Not many C.Os would have bought P/O stripes, D.F.C. and D.F.M ribbons in advance, knowing these items were unobtainable in Malta.

In spite of the presence in Malta of many people who were not on the side of the Allies there seemed to be very few attempts at sabotage during my ten months on the island. One positive occasion which affected the P.R. Spitfires was when the early-morning aircraft on the 'milk-run' was being prepared for flight. About an hour before dawn an eagle-eyed airman found a heavy rag stuffed into the oil cooler on the underside of the aircraft. If it had taken off, the oil temperature would have risen beyond the maximum five or six minutes later, some twenty miles out at sea. The pilot might have survived but the Spitfire would certainly have been lost.

I was involved in what may have been another possible sabotage attempt. One of our regular tasks was for photographic coverage of the many airfields and seaplane bases in the Rome/Naples area. This involved a long flight of about five hours and the pilot did not have much fuel on board on his return. I was tasked for this in March 1943 and had a successful trip until I was about 150 miles from home. I had reached the Straits of Messina between Sicily and the toe of Italy and was studying the local area from about 25,000 feet for any enemy interference, when the slight flicker of a red light caught my attention. I watched the cockpit dials and indicators for a few moments and saw another flicker of red light. It was the fuel pressure warning light. The fuel contents gauge showed that I had about forty minutes fuel left so it could not be lack of petrol. After a minute or so the red light came on and stayed on for a few seconds and the engine coughed once or twice. Shortly, the light came on and stayed on for half a minute and the engine failed during that whole period. I was now losing height and had the unpleasant thought that I still had to pass over the three enemy fighter stations situated on the south coast of Sicily.

I realised that the fuel pressure failure must be due to some obstruction in the system, very likely a clogged filter somewhere. It was clearly essential to regain pressure somehow and the only course open to me was to reduce height and increase atmospheric pressure. Normally unwise, however in this case it was unavoidable. I had to keep the engine ticking over until I had passed the enemy airfields. I crossed the Sicilian coast at about 4,000 ft. with the engine occasionally picking up and giving a burst of power. I am sure the 'duck egg blue' colour of our P.R. Spitfires helped me to return to friendly skies that day because I was not attacked – perhaps not even seen. The last 50 miles were a nightmare with the engine picking up for a moment or so then failing. At last I saw the outline of the island ahead and landed safely.

But that was not the end of the story. The aircraft fuel system was inspected and found to contain sand. The filter in the main tank was almost completely blocked. The system was thoroughly flushed out, tested and found serviceable once again. The aircraft was refuelled, air tested and flown on various sorties during the next few days without any further trouble.

It so happened that the next routine coverage of the Rome/Naples airfields fell to me again and I was given the same aircraft. I am sure this was just the luck of the draw. I completed the photographic task and was homeward bound when, as I passed over Stromboli (a perfect example of a volcano and always exuding a trail of white smoke from the crater) I noticed a flicker of red from that same warning light. Oh, not again, I thought and watched the indicator carefully. Sure enough, a while later the light came on again, this time for a second or two. The sequence of events occurred as before and I started to lose height to increase atmospheric pressure. This time I had two important advantages – I knew this time what the problem was, and secondly the weather over Sicily was quite different from the previous time. The island was scattered with clouds, some of which were heavy and stormy. At least if I could keep going I could hide from fighters by flying in cloud.

By the time I approached the south coast of Sicily I was down to 5,000 ft. and in and out of cloud, the engine cutting out frequently. I knew I would have difficulty reaching Malta, 60 miles away, so I declared an emergency on the radio and requested assistance. A strange but thoroughly English voice replied immediately and instructed me to turn on to a westerly heading, continue my descent and look out for the island. The directions he gave me didn't make sense – I could see Sicily's south coast below me and I knew that Malta was south of my position – so I took no notice. Then the voice of the Malta controller told me to maintain my present heading and stated that a section of fighters had been directed to escort me back to base. Neither enemy nor friendly fighters found me that day.

Things were getting desperate. I was down to 2,000 ft. over the sea with the engine idling when it suddenly occurred to me that the 'primer pump' (which pushes fuel directly into the engine for starting up) might save the day. I made the last thirty miles on that primer, exhausted by having to pump left handed while keeping airborne with my right hand on the control column. The Kigas priming pump saved my bacon that day but I sometimes wondered how the sand managed to get into the fuel system in the first place.

I remember a remarkable incident, which occurred towards the end of my tour of operations on the island. The invasion of Sicily had been planned and was imminent. A very large number of aircraft was based on R.A.F. Luqa in readiness for the big day and among them were two or three Tomahawk and Kittyhawk fighter-bomber Squadrons whose immediate task was to bomb and strafe the enemy fighter stations in southern Sicily, e.g. Comiso, Gela, and Castelvetrano. One beautiful, warm, sunny day just about noon a Kittyhawk Squadron taxied past our office. We sometimes had a chance to watch these operations if we were not tasked ourselves. Eleven aircraft, fully bombed up, lined up and prepared for take-off. A minute later a twelfth Kittyhawk taxied by, emitting black smoke and sounding very rough. The pilot seemed unaware of, or unperturbed, by the state of the engine and pressed on. Eleven aircraft took off and disappeared to the North. Tail-end Charlie revved up at the end of the runway and, to everyone's surprise took off and followed his colleagues, using the entire runway, still belching smoke and sounding like a broken sewing machine – tapokka-tapokka-tapokka…

We all thought, "There goes a brave chap, stupid, but brave". Some thirty minutes later the eleven Kittyhawks in the first 'wave' came back, circled the airfield, landed, and taxied back to their dispersal. Another twenty minutes went by and we regretfully decided that 'Charlie' in the second 'wave' was lost. A courageous but foolhardy pilot. But no. A small speck appeared in the sky to the North, trailing smoke all the way. The aircraft circled and landed, minus his bomb, still belching black smoke and sounding terrible. We heard later that the pilot stated on his return that, "he didn't think the aircraft had performed particularly well that day and maybe someone ought to check the plugs".

You don't often see an R.A.F. man with an Army medal. One of my colleagues on 683 Squadron, Sgt. Micky Tardiff, failed to return from one of the 'milk-run' missions to the Italian naval bases. We heard later that having taken off at 11 o'clock for the noon run he had reached the Italian coast near Crotone when his engine began to overheat due to a small leak in the coolant tank. Micky knew he would have to bail out when the engine seized. He did so a few minutes later and landed in scrub country near the coast. He buried his parachute and managed to evade capture for two days. Unluckily, he was seen by a search party and was imprisoned in Taranto – one of his targets.

Some weeks later the prisoners held in the gaol were put on board a train en-route for Germany and the P.O.W. camps. The journey was frequently interrupted by allied strafing raids and on one of the occasions when the train ground to a halt, Micky evaded the guards and jumped off the train. He managed to escape into the hills and soon met up with a group of partisans operating against the German and Italian road convoys in the district. They would pick off the last truck in the convoy and make off before the leading vehicles were aware of their loss. Tardiff stayed with the group for many months, eventually being chosen as their leader, until the invading Allies reached the area. On one occasion he was hiding from a German patrol which was searching for the partisans and the daughter of the house where he lived urged him to take to his bed and feign illness. She then told the German officer that he was her brother and was suffering from malaria. (Micky Tardiff was a Channel Islander and, luckily for him and also for the daughter, was of a somewhat swarthy complexion.) The German accepted the explanation and left.

Micky was very well liked and looked after by the local people and they were sorry to lose their 'Capitaine Mickey' when he eventually left them to re-join the Allied Services. Sometime later he was awarded the Military Medal for his exploits, a gong which was richly deserved.

The principal duty of photographic reconnaissance in wartime is to provide up-to-date information to the Commanders of the fighting forces. The efforts of the ground-crews and aircrews are vital to this end but their contribution would be of little value if it were not for the photo interpreters who spent hours poring over the films brought back from the aircrews and then writing full reports on their findings.

I recall one particular instance of the tremendous ability of these unsung heroes. One of our aircraft had taken routine photos of the harbour and airfield at Palermo, the Sicilian capital on the north coast of the island. The interpreters noticed construction activity in one obscure corner of the harbour where, in peace time, fishing boats were built and repaired. They asked us to keep an occasional eye on the area and for the next few weeks we made sure that photo coverage of Palermo was on the agenda. Time came when even the pilots realised that something exceptional was happening down there. The interpreters explained that a light cruiser was being built and that in a few weeks it would be put to sea on its trial. When we queried them on this startling information they pointed to some minute objects on the quayside. "Those are piles of seamen's kitbags waiting to go on board. You can also see a fuzzy haze on the photograph which indicates that the engines are being tested. In a day or so we shall see trunks and suitcases on the dockside when the officers will be going aboard. There'll be a settling-in period and then she'll be away."

We photographed the ship two or three times a day from then on – any pilot who had a task which took him anywhere near Palermo would divert there to get a picture. At last the time came when the interpreters said they expected the cruiser to be put to sea on its trials on a particular night. We doubled our coverage and the day came at last. The cruiser was sunk that night by a British submarine which had been lying in wait three miles outside Palermo harbour.

Flying operations from Malta were not always filled with excitement and alarm. There were quiet periods occasionally....

I had taken off from R.A.F. Luqa for a task in North Africa, 200 miles away, and was climbing through about 10,000 ft. when I saw a speck in the sky ahead of me. Always ready to turn away and run from a possible unfriendly aircraft, I delayed for a few seconds to confirm my sighting. It turned out to be an eagle. How wonderful to meet up with a lonely traveller going about his own peaceful affairs, migrating from Europe to Africa. Sadly, he took no notice of me; after all, the king of the skies fears no-one.

On another flight, again to North Africa, I was scheduled for a pre-dawn take-off so that I could arrive at my coastal targets, 200 miles away, at first photographic light. They were located on both sides of the coast road east of Tripoli where Rommel's German and Italian troops were expected to try to make a stand. Photographic cover of any major moves or preparations the enemy might make was essential. I had climbed to 25,000 ft. in the half light of a Mediterranean dawn and as I looked out to the east I saw the tip of the rising sun creeping above the horizon. There was a layer of broken cumulus cloud lying low down over the sea and their tops were being painted by rays of bright gold as the sun rose out of the sea. It was truly beautiful.

44

Cloud over the target was much lower than forecast so I had to make a rapid descent to get the necessary pictures. When my work was completed I decided to evacuate the area at low level until well out to sea on my return to Malta. From about 200 ft. above the waves I glanced towards the east and saw another sunrise, this time a richer, deeper gold shining from the rising sun which lit up the bottom layers of the puffy clouds.

I had seen two sunrises, each outstandingly beautiful. My Merlin engine was running sweetly, the Axis enemy was being forced out of the African continent and one could therefore reasonably hope that the end of the war in the Mediterranean theatre was in sight. My return to base was made just in and below the low cloud base where an impression of very high speed could be achieved which enhanced even more my feeling of satisfaction at the way things were developing. All seemed well with the world.

The Royal Navy and the Royal Air Force worked very closely together throughout the conflict in the Mediterranean. Between them, their two main aims were (i) to protect as far as possible the Allied convoys moving to and from Alexandria and Gibraltar and (ii) to try to prevent movement of supplies especially high octane fuel for tanks and aircraft from Axis-held ports in southern Europe to Rommel's German and Italian forces in North Africa.

In my particular case I rarely came into direct contact with the Navy but I did spend two exciting days in the company of one of their smaller Units....

On the 22nd January, about ten weeks after Operation Torch began (the Allied invasion of North Africa from Gibraltar), I was briefed to fly to the Tunis/Bizerte region of Tunisia to photograph and make a written report on the airfields, harbours, railway marshalling yards and shipping movements. I was required to take off at 11:00 hrs so I had an early lunch which turned out to be of tinned fish (a very rare delicacy) and 'duff', an amalgam of flour and, I think, pulverised ships' biscuits which was our staple diet. Amazing, the number of ways that duff could be prepared to provide the foundation of every meal!

I took off on time and climbed to 25,000 ft. Shortly before reaching my targets I began to feel decidedly uncomfortable with stomach pains and profound rumblings. This discomfort increased rapidly as I carried out my photo work and scribbled my reports of the Tunis area.

45

I realised that I would find it very difficult, if not impossible, to navigate my way over 200 miles of sea back to Malta. My briefing had included mention of the Allied forces advancing from the West and that parts of Algeria were already in Allied hands. So I headed west and searched for the first available airfield which had British or American aircraft on it. It turned out to be Bone (now Annaba), in Algeria, where a number of Swordfish aeroplanes were dispersed. I landed and was soon able to sort out my personal problems. There was no way I could return to Malta that day, a decision that was strongly seconded by the Naval Medico. The photos and my written report could not be flown back to Malta because all the serviceable Swordfish aircraft were loaded with under-slung torpedoes and were being prepared for a full-scale shipping attack that night along the enemy's coastal waters. For my part, I would have been perfectly happy to consign the whole lot to the waves which were close by.

As it happened, a curious and most fortunate coincidence was about to take place which was to solve the problem. A photo-reconnaissance Mosquito aircraft had taken off from R.A.F. Benson in Oxfordshire some hours before with the task of photographing large areas of Sardinia to facilitate the planning for the possible future invasion of that island. The pilot and navigator were happily engaged on this mosaic exercise when one of their engines failed. A return to Benson over enemy territory on one engine was out of the question so they decided to head for the nearest Allied airfield on the African coast – Bone in Algeria. So now we had two beautiful blue P.R. aeroplanes stranded on a small airfield in Africa which was occupied by the Royal Navy flying the gallant Swordfish.

The coincidence didn't stop there. The Mosquito pilot, Paul Ritchie, whose name I remember after sixty years, had flown Spitfires before and was keen to get his hands on one again. It was a simple matter to refuel the Spitfire, load his films from the Mosquito and disappear to the east.

Back in Malta all anybody knew was that a Spitfire BS 364 with me on board had taken off at 11 o'clock to go to Tunisia. It was now half past five, long past the maximum period that even a P.R. Spitfire could stay airborne. "He's had it. Engine failure or been shot down. Ah well, that's the way it goes."

Then, ten minutes later, a blue Spitfire lands and taxies up to the dispersal. It is BS 364 for sure but the wrong pilot gets out!

Back at Bone, Paul Ritchie's navigator and I watched the Navy boys' activities in preparing for the night's operations and when dusk fell all the serviceable Swordfish got airborne and disappeared towards the coast. We had been given pup tents to sleep in but just when darkness came down and it became quiet again the airfield was attacked by German fighter bombers. The enemy was suffering badly in the North African campaign from lack of arms, ammunition, fuel and other supplies. Their shipping convoys from Europe were being decimated by attacks from allied forces such as the Swordfish Squadron at Bone and the powerful naval and air Units based in Malta. No wonder the Axis forces took every chance to retaliate… but, I thought, why choose a night when I was there?

I had never felt so naked, so vulnerable, and so helpless when the bombs fell. Only a thin skin of canvas between me and the explosions. The excitement was intense! Fortunately, no damage was done in this raid to personnel, buildings or equipment. Two days later about noon a Spitfire arrives, flown by a very happy-looking Mosquito pilot. "They won't believe me when I get back to Benson. They'll be jealous as Hell."

I thanked and said farewell to my Naval hosts, bought a few dozen oranges from an Arab trader and returned to Luqa at 30,000ft to freeze them. A rapid descent to base ensured they would remain frozen until the ground crews could get at them. The Squadron 'chiefy' Flight Sergeant Gadsby and Sergeant Pass, our instrument 'basher', asked if I would please repeat the exercise the next time I went to the African coast – the oranges were superb. I told them, "Sorry, no chance, it is far too dangerous there – much safer here in Malta".

# 10. Poor Standard Of Shipping Recognition

DURING EACH PRE-FLIGHT briefing we received a reminder to report immediately, by radio, if any large merchant vessels or warships were sighted at sea. Especially important in this regard were tankers, wherever they were, wherever they were heading. I noted this in my logbook for future reference.

I had climbed to 25,000 ft. on my way to Taranto and Brindisi on the heel of Italy. At this operating height there was an extensive and thick layer of milky cirrus cloud ideal for hiding from the enemy. As I flew up to Cape Spartivento at the tow of Italy I saw below me a large vessel, easily recognisable as a tanker – with pipes lying fore and aft along the deck – hugging the coast and proceeding south, just the type of sighting mentioned in the briefing. I made a radio call stating its position, speed and heading. I also took photographs to confirm my report though I thought at the time they would not be very clear because of the hazy cirrus. I then carried on with my task.

The authorities in Malta acted immediately on my radio call and a couple of Fishingtons (torpedo-carrying Wellingtons) were scrambled. They found the ship and sank it, fortunately without damage to themselves. I say 'fortunately', not for the obvious reasons, but because my tanker turned out to be a large coasting vessel carrying a deck cargo of tree trunks and I would have been even more mortified if either of our aircraft had been lost. I have often wondered what the Italian ship's Captain must have thought, to have been 'honoured' by the attention of the two attackers. I was 'carpeted' for this performance and my logbook was endorsed – presumably for poor standard of shipping recognition.

On a subsequent occasion I was photographing the airfields, ports and railway marshalling yards in the Rome/Naples area and I found well over a hundred JU 52 transport aircraft on the airfield at Pomigliano d'Arco, near Naples. It was clear that the Germans were now trying to supply Rommel by air when their efforts by sea were less than successful. My sightings and photographs were reinforced later that day when scores of these aircraft were seen at Trapani airfield in the west of Sicily.

This army of transports was strongly attacked by all available aircraft from Malta and dozens of the JU 52s were shot down. Some of the fighter pilots reported return fire from the windows of the transports by soldiers firing tommy guns. They didn't stand a chance, especially when the aircraft crashed into the sea on fire – they had been carrying aviation fuel stored in 45 gallon drums. Very few of the hundred-odd transports reached the airfields on the north coast of Africa.

A gripping account of this period can be studied in Tony Spooner's 'Conspicuous Gallantry'.

It seems that my below average ability in ship recognition and any other misdemeanours that I committed in the air were forgiven by the powers that be because in February of 1943 I was awarded the DFM (Distinguished Flying Medal) and I attended an investiture in Valetta, Malta's battered capital, to receive the honour from Viscount Lord Gort, VC. the Viceroy at that time.

By August that year I had done 350 hours of operational flying and my tour of duty was complete. I elected to return to the U.K., largely because the successful invasion of Sicily and then Italy meant that Malta's position as the hub of the Mediterranean theatre of war would be lost, and the centre of activity would drift northwards with the Allies' advance in that direction. I was sorry to leave Malta and the very many friends I had made there. Years later, just before I left the Royal Air Force, I was there again for a too-short visit. The Maltese folk I had known in those difficult days were still there and it was clear they were still staunchly supportive of British traditions and the British way of life.

Early in 1944, I was sitting in the Officers' Mess anteroom in the R.A.F. Station at Dyce, near Aberdeen. I was idly glancing through a rather dilapidated copy of The London Illustrated News whilst waiting for transport back to the base for the afternoon's flying when I came across a photograph which I recognised. It showed a minor naval action in the Mediterranean just off the toe of Italy. The caption stated that a photo-recce pilot had "snapped" the picture of a successful attack on an Italian vessel. Memories returned... I had been returning to Malta from one of the 'milk-run' sorties and had just finished photographing the harbour at Messina where three Italian cruisers were clearly visible form my height of 25,000 ft. I was casually searching the area around me for possible enemy threats when my attention was drawn to a commotion in the sea some fifteen miles ahead. I could see a large ship which was slowly breaking in two amidships. As I came closer I saw a destroyer and some Motor Torpedo Boats firing depth charges all around the scene. A Cant Seaplane was flying low over the sea, clearly carrying out a search. I made a photo-run over the scene from about 20,000 ft. and then watched as the stricken vessel disappeared beneath the waves. My report back at base was a little more interesting this time than the usual one recording the fact that the big Italian warships were safely in dock and thus posed no threat to our convoys from Alexandria and Gibraltar.

There was a sequel to this incident. The commander of the British submarine which sank the ship had to lie low, resting on the sea bed while the search and the attacks continued against him. He had no opportunity to confirm whether his torpedo attack had been successful. On his return to Malta some days later to refuel and rearm he was presented with photographic evidence of the success he had hoped for.

# 11. An Officer And A Gentleman

I RETURNED TO THE U.K. by air on August 24th 1943.

My next posting, to R.A.F. Dyce, turned out to be the most important period of my life for it was there that I met the delightful person who was to become my wife; but more of that anon.

During my absence, Malta No. 8 (Coastal) O.C.U. had been moved from Fraserburgh to Dyce where some specially converted Mosquito aircraft had been added to the Photo Recce 'empire'. Dyce was quite busy with Masters for the Spitfire conversion Squadron, Mosquitos and various Marks of Spitfires. Two or three early types of Spits were used for 'first solo' flights. I suppose they were deemed expendable, they were no longer used in Fighter Command. It was easy to recognise a 'first soloist' because the Spitfire I and II had an undercarriage system operated by a pump in the cockpit. This pump was located in the right-hand side of the cockpit and the pilot had to change hands to raise the wheels just after take-off. The left hand, normally busy with the throttle; mixture and pitch controls; flap and engine levers, was now required to hold the aircraft steady while the right hand struggled with the pump. The poor aircraft climbed away in a serried of steps.

It was standard procedure, and a very sensible one at that, I think, for tour-expired aircrews to be made available to join the staffs at the Operations Conversion Units, mainly to pass on their own experiences and techniques to the newcomers who would shortly be flying operationally. The main requirement for those chosen for this appointment is the ability to instruct.

The number of Units devoted to the task of producing instructors was limited and, for pilots, was supervised by the Central Flying School (CFS), the father Unit for teaching how to instruct.

In my case I was sent to No. 3 Flying Instructor School at R.A.F. Lulsgate Bottom, (in spite of its name it was built on high ground) near Bristol. I completed just over 40 hours of day and night flying on Master aircraft and emerged with an instructional category of Q (S/E) which meant I was qualified to instruct on single-engine aircraft. I spent the next seven months at Dyce which is now Aberdeen's civil airport.

My duties at Dyce were fairly straightforward. I was responsible for checking out, on Master aircraft, the qualified pilots allotted to me who had now joined the P.R.O.C.U. Their conversion to the Spitfires would follow and then the techniques of a P.R. pilot would be explained and practised e.g. pilot navigation (of extreme importance), instrument flying, the uses of various types of camera etc.

One of my students was a Nigerian whose father, a Chief in his homeland, had provided funds to buy Spitfires for the war effort. It was therefore natural that the father would hope, even expect, that his son who was already a pilot would fly a Spitfire. Peter John Emanuel Adeniyi Thomas, had a considerable amount of flying time on Masters but his reaction time in practice emergencies were slow and basically unsafe. After the standard instructional time had been completed I considered that he was not yet fit to fly the Spitfire – it would be too fast for him. The Chief Flying Instructor authorised additional flying time for him but when that was completed the standard achieved was still not good enough.

It was perhaps unfortunate that the requirement for Peter Thomas to fly a Spitfire was a political matter and the Foreign Office kept an eye on his progress. He was posted away for further flying experience on Masters and eventually returned to Dyce for P.R. operational training. We were very happy to have him back as he had a delightful personality – he was also a wonderful drummer in the station band.

In spite of further instruction from me and additional solo work I found it quite impossible to authorise him to go solo on the Spitfire for the same reasons as before. He had reached his peak on the slower and less sophisticated aircraft. The Flight Commander flew with him and agreed with my recommendation that he should not be permitted to fly Spitfires or any aircraft more advanced that the Master. The Foreign Office was advised accordingly and Peter Thomas was sent to some other Spitfire conversion Unit. He was killed when he lost control on his first Spitfire flight. I cannot help thinking this was a case of misplaced political expediency.

One day I was asked to fly the Station Padre to Fraserburgh where he was to officiate at a funeral. During the service I passed the time in the Officers' Mess getting up to date with local and national news. When the Padre was ready to return to Dyce we went out to the aeroplane and prepared for the flight. I completed the external checks and helped my passenger to climb into the rear cockpit and to do up his safety straps.

I must make it clear that the undercarriage system on the Master II was unique. The UP/DOWN lever, located along the left hand side of each cockpit, was safeguarded against accidental operation by a heavy spring and there was a 'neutral' position for the lever between the UP and DOWN positions of the selector. When the pilot wished to raise the wheels after take-off he would grasp the selector handle, pull hard backwards to release it from the spring and then move it to the UP position. The wheels would then retract into the body of the aircraft. The reverse movement of the selector lever would allow the wheels to be lowered for landing. It was the aircraft captain's responsibility to ensure that the undercarriage selector was in the DOWN position whenever the aircraft was about to land or was on the ground taxying. The heavy spring ensured that the lever would stay firmly in the selected position. The whole system was operated by an engine driven pump.

When I started up the engine the aircraft moved forward about a foot and then gently sank to the ground, ruining the three-blade propeller and damaging the under surface of the fuselage. No doubt the engine had been shock-loaded as well. I was utterly confounded. After a moment a quick check of the cockpit revealed that the lever had moved to the UP position despite the heavy spring. How and when it happened was only of importance to me. I was the responsible person. We made an ignominious return to Dyce – at least, I did. I just hoped the Padre would pray for heavenly guidance for me at the forthcoming Inquiry.

Some months later, just before I returned to my second tour of operations, I was required to report to the Air Officer Commanding (A.O.C.) at Group Headquarters in Kent. The long railway journey did nothing to reduce the trepidation I felt. It was even worse when I arrived at my destination. I found that the waiting room was filled with aircrews who had, in one way or another, been judged responsible for damage to aircraft or equipment. We questioned one another as to the misdemeanour he was 'up for' and, as each one came away from the A.O.C.'s office we realised that even very minor infringements such as slight damage to a wingtip during taxying were 'visited' with severe reprimands and, in some cases, loss of seniority (equivalent to a heavy fine). My crime was by far the most serious and I expected the worst, naturally. At least, I couldn't be shot at dawn, surely. When I entered the A.O.C.'s office he was glowering at the reports on my incident. I saluted and stated, "Flying Officer Durbidge, Sir, reporting". He was silent for a long, long minute and my heart sank. He then looked up at me under dark, heavy brows. "Durbidge," he said, "You're a bloody fool". I said "Yes, Sir". Another pause. "What did you say?" I said , "Sir, I agreed with you. I was a bloody fool". A very long pause ensued. "Durbidge, I was a B.F., like you, a long time ago". He then proceeded to tell me his life story of flying in the R.A.F. Finally he said, "Get out of my office. I don't want to see you here again". I got out.

The pilots in the waiting room had stayed behind to hear my sentence and, thanks possibly to the Padre, I was able to tell them, "Oh, we discussed flying as a career, though he did most of the talking".

Sometimes the airfield would be invaded by a haar, a sea fog which developed over the North Sea and drifted inland. When this occurred flying would be called off and the instructors would be engaged in briefings or lectures to the students or in writing up their reports. On one such occasion a few of us were relaxing playing liar dice and hoping the fog would clear. The Station Adjutant, (I forget his name though I shouldn't for reasons that will soon be clear) came to the crew room and announced the he wanted a few volunteers for a worthwhile cause. He said that he'd received a letter from a school in Aberdeen asking if the Station could provide a few pilots to talk about their war experiences to a Boys Club which had been organised by one or two of the teachers. The aim was to keep them off the streets, especially during a period when Aberdeen was being subjected to bombing attacks by the Luftwaffe. The request was for one speaker each week for a few weeks to talk to the boys starting at 8:00 p.m.

We said, "O.K. Adj, No problem, Adj, Count us in, Adj, etc.," hoping he would go away and leave us alone. We thought no more about it but he remembered those who had volunteered. He wrote back to the school accordingly. A week or so later the Adjutant came to the Flight and said, "Right now, about this Boys Club lecture thing. You, Johnny, are on tonight at 20.00 hours and here's the address. You're on next week Keith, and Snowy, you're talking the week after. If they want any more I'll let you know who goes when".

Nonplussed was not the word for it. We'd forgotten completely. The Adj hadn't. However, Pilot Officer Johnson said he'd take his dog with him to keep the 'monsters' in order if necessary. The animal in question was about as big as a small cat but maybe Johnny would be able to control it and the boys as well.

The following week I was reminded by the Adjutant that it was my turn and Johnny agreed to show me how to get to the school in the blackout – he was going into town anyway, to see a movie. Two very pleasant young ladies who ran the Club welcomed me in for my stint. The talk went quite well and I said that an Australian pilot would be along the next time.

When Snowy's time came it was a very dark night and I offered to show him where to go – I planned to visit the cinema anyway. The door was opened by one of the teachers and I introduced Snowy. She said, "How lucky to have you both here because we have an extra group of boys here tonight. Perhaps you'd be kind enough to repeat your talk from last week to the new ones?" What could an officer and a gentleman say? When we finished that evening Snowy, who had taken a shine to Lorna, said, "Why don't we go down to the Caley (Caledonian Hotel & Bar) for a drink?" That was the start of my association with Elsie McKay (her family and friends called her Bunty so I had to follow suit once I got used to it). We had a mutual interest in classical music and plays, and Aberdeen provided a remarkably good supply of both for a wartime situation. Warwick Braithwaite was the regular conductor of the Scottish Symphony Orchestra and they presented monthly programmes of good music and the King's theatre often offered plays prior to their London debut.

Bunty was a teacher in Aberdeen and I was about to return for my next operational tour to R.A.F. Benson, near Oxford, the home of Photographic Reconnaissance. We could not be much further apart and, of course, wartime travelling opportunities and conditions made for very irregular meetings, however much we tried. Every chance we had we took. I managed to meet Bunty's family and she met mine. It didn't take us long to agree to get married and ten months after I left Dyce we took the plunge. We must have done the right thing because we celebrated our 60th wedding anniversary in April 2005.

Operational flying from Benson was quite different from that which I had experienced in the Mediterranean. For example; visibility from height was much impaired by industrial pollution; the weather, generally, was more changeable and less predictable; the absence of large areas of sea and associated coastlines made navigation much less straightforward and reduced the P.R. pilot's usual method of escape from attack; the Germans were now on their own and seemed, to me anyway, to be more determined and positive, and better organised; and their anti-aircraft defences were more accurate. On the other hand, instead of having one very small area and one airfield to return to if you were in difficulty there were scores of safe havens in the U.K.

I found that the type of target for photo recce was also very much changed. Large areas of forest in Northern France were regularly photographed in the search for V.1 and V.2 rocket sires. Bomb damage assessment sorties determined the effect of the heavy bombing programme by Bomber Command at night, the Americans by day were a daily requirement and of course the number of standard targets such as harbours, airfields, oil refineries and railway systems from Northern Norway to the Spanish border were regularly covered. Benson had two Spitfire and two Mosquito Squadrons for this enormous task and they were permanently busy.

Benson was a typical southern English village with one church and seven pubs. The E.A.P. Station impinged on the village and was the dominating factor in its life. It was busy, with aircraft noises and smells and most of the local talk was of aeroplanes. The pubs filled up at night with thirsty airmen and airwomen from the very early days of the war. There were few shops and most of the tradesmen came from nearby Wallingford, a small town on the Thames. The station was the home of photographic reconnaissance throughout the war and for some years afterwards. At one time it also housed the Queen's Flight in one of the hangers. I wonder if that hangar's floor is still polished. Can you imagine polishing concrete?

I joined No. 542 Spitfire P.R. Squadron at Benson in June 1944 just after the D-Day landings. We were equipped with Spitfire P.R. Mk X and XI aircraft with the Merlin 63 engines which burned a gallon of fuel per minute and gave us five hours safe airborne time, over six hours if we carried 90-gallon drop tanks. (This enormous tank which, of course, was used up first, cleared the ground on take-off by about six inches. We kept it on board, even when empty, until we were over a German town, hoping that, during its descent it might knock some Nazi sympathiser on the head.)

The Mk. X aircraft was fitted with a partly pressurised cockpit which didn't really please all the pilots. It had been thought to be an advantage since most of our work was done at high altitude. It was heavier of course, but the main disadvantage was its instability. I found that I spent more time trimming the controls to maintain fore-and-aft steadiness during the climb, and especially during prolonged photographic runs, than I spent attending to other tasks.

In the last year of the war we were equipped with the Mk. 19 with the Griffon engine driving a five-bladed propeller, which rotated in the opposite direction to the earlier Spitfires. This was a truly remarkable beast. The torque effect of this powerful combination caught many a pilot on his first take-off. I saw a Mk. 19 get airborne once and the pilot either opened the throttle too quickly or failed to apply full right rudder – the Spit left the runway and disappeared behind the hanger at about 50ft. before the pilot realised what was happening. Once airborne though it was a dream, but I never did really get used to the popping, crackling and banging noise which occurred when the Griffon was throttled back during the landing procedure. However I consider that I very likely owe my life to the Griffon engine. One morning I was tasked to carry out a bomb damage assessment sortie over the Ruhr at 11.00 hours.

There had been an attack by a force of about 50 American Fortress bombers escorted by Mustang fighters. The previous night the same target area, in Germany's industrial heartland, had been bombed by R.A.F. Bomber Command and it was hoped that the photographs would confirm that particular part of the Ruhr would not need further attention for some time.

I carried out a number of runs over the smoking ruins from 25,000ft producing a mosaic of the target area. I set course for home and about fifteen minutes later, as I was approaching the Dutch border, I saw ahead of me an armada of heavy aircraft coming straight for me about my height. Our closing speed must have been around 600 mph; I had no time to turn away from the mass of aircraft. I recognised Fortresses and Mustangs. They were, thankfully, the bomber force whose results I was sent to photograph but they had been postponed by some hours and nobody had told the operations staff at Benson.

I flew through the mass of aeroplanes and I must have looked like a strange-coloured German aircraft, the Me 109, because at least one Mustang, high above the bombers, peeled off and dived towards me. With his height advantage he soon caught me up. I'd had experience before of the poor standard of aircraft recognition of American fighter pilots so I had no hesitation in putting on the full power of the Griffon and easing the stick back for a maximum rate climb. I left him behind within a minute and returned to base. I may not have been as lucky had I been in a Mk. XI Spitfire.

Despite the speed of the Griffon engine, the Mk. XI was still a wonderful machine and although sitting on a rubber cushion which was on a rubber dinghy which was on a parachute, for five hours or more was a bit of a bind (in more ways than one) the delight in flying a Spitfire more than outweighed the discomfort. Of course, one of the requisites for a P.R. pilot was an accommodating bladder – there was no pilot relief tube.

I recall one particular sortie which took over 5 ½ hours. I had been briefed to fly to Berlin and cover half the city after a Bomber attack the previous night. Another pilot was briefed to complete the other half of the mosaic. The task involved making seven long runs each for a full coverage. The weather was good and I had no interference of any kind while I was over Berlin. I saw the other aircraft flying to and fro, clearly getting on with his task. When I got back to Benson I learned that my colleague in the other aircraft had needed to return to base with engine trouble and there had been no chance to fly the sortie that day. So it was an enemy aircraft that had been flying around near me. I am sure that our duck-egg blue camouflage was well chosen to help make us invisible.

I didn't really enjoy making mosaics over enemy territory – I don't think anyone did – because most of your time is spent adjusting the camera controls at the start of each run; holding a steady compass course throughout the run; and keeping track of your exact position at the beginning and end of every run, leaving you very little time to keep a look-out for any opportunities.

Some of the most difficult and least rewarding sorties were those flown to find the launching sites of the V1 and V2 weapons. They were called No-balls and Cross-bows and we were given large chunks of French forest, which looked just like any other French forest, and the road systems serving the area didn't help, being metalled (crushed rocks used for the road surfaces) on the maps and un-metalled when you got there. The launch sites were extremely well camouflaged and it was only when the branches of the trees, which were used to cover the ramps, died off that the cameras could pick out the differences from the surrounding woods.

Speaking of camouflage, a story is told, and it could be true, that when the Germans built a new jet airfield near the French north coast they paid particular attention to camouflaging their activities. Its progress was monitored by Benson. At the same time, to divert attention, they built a wooden airfield, complete with wooden aircraft and buildings, about five miles away, clearly hoping that one would be noticed and attacked while the real target would be left alone. Apparently, when the jet airfield became operational it was heavily bombed and virtually destroyed. A wooden bomb was dropped on the decoy.

Incidentally, there is a small Dutch grass airfield named De Kooy which I have photographed but, as far as I know, it was never used operationally by the Germans. Maybe they didn't know it was there or perhaps the Dutch used it as a decoy?

About half way back from one of these long-range flights I noticed, straight ahead of me, a dark streak of smoke which appeared to shoot up from the ground. I had seen nothing like this before so I watched it carefully. It soon became clear that it was the rocket exhaust from a Messerschmitt 163, one of the latest weapons in the German armoury. The machine reached my height of 25,000 ft. in a very short time and began to circle round in my direction. I knew its speed to be extremely high though I had no idea of its manoeuvrability. It came round behind me a few miles off and seemed to turn in my direction, clearly under control from the ground. Fascinating as it was, this was no time to study it.

I decided that he would be within firing range in 15 seconds. By good fortune there was a patch of stratus cloud about 1,000 ft. ahead and below me so I dived into it and spent the next ten minutes circling around. I knew that the ME 163 had a very short rocket-endurance engine and that he would not be able to wait around for me to re-appear so I emerged from the cloud and pressed on home. It was at least ten more years before I was able to study it carefully – in an aircraft museum.

Any flights from Benson to the northern parts of Germany, like Hamburg, Kiel, and Wilhelmshaven would pass along the Frisian Islands (also known as Wadden Islands) which are strewn in a long chain from the Dutch north coast at Texel to the mouth of the Weser at Bremerhaven. The Germans had placed some anti-aircraft guns along this chain and they were operated by experienced naval gunners. They must have been radar-assisted because they always seemed to get our height right straight away. Invariably, there would be a puff of smoke when the shell burst, spot on for height but way behind the aircraft by a mile or so. The next burst would be much nearer and we used to advise new pilots to watch out for this in the rear-view mirror. We recommended that the third shot, about a quarter of a mile behind, signalled the time to turn away sharply left or right. Sure enough the fourth shell would explode just about where you would have been had you not turned away. You then carried on with your flight watching for the next series of shells.

One of our squadron members, David Rutherford, whom I had known as a student at Dyce just before I left there, was briefed for a flight to the North German coastal area. He was warned about the German gunners along the Frisians but he did not return from his sortie. He became a prisoner of war and when he came back in June 1945 we asked him what had happened. He said that everything had occurred as we forecast, he saw the first burst in his mirror, watched for the second and the third bursts and then turned hard right to avoid the fourth. The fourth went straight through his engine, slap bang amidships. No choice but to bail out and spend the rest of the war behind prison walls. You can't win 'em all – at least he was lucky in that the shell went straight through the engine without exploding or it could have been a different story.

I remember taking the same route along the Frisians when I had targets in Denmark and Northern Germany. There was plenty of high cirrus cloud at my height and the hazy conditions made accurate map reading difficult. I had just made out Heligoland away on my left and I said to myself that I should see the German coast in a minute or so and a voice said, "Ought to see the German coast any minute now". Somewhat shaken, I looked all around in the haze and thought, "Ah, there it is".

The same voice said, "There it is, down there, ahead". Now I knew that I was crazy to be flying with a gremlin in my radio. However, that someone had inadvertently left his radio transmitter switched on was the only reasonable explanation. This was a dangerous thing to do over enemy territory so I made one attempt to warn him but of course he would not be able to get my message with his transmitter still on. It turned out to be a P.R. Mosquito off to photograph Kiel, Lübeck and Hamburg. I was glad to learn later that the crew had returned safely.

Late on in the war, during the bitter winter of 1944-45 when freezing fog affected most of England, R.A.F. Benson – which was situated on a very gentle slope – was being used as a diversion airfield for many of the U.S.A.F. bomber squadrons returning from daylight operations. A few Mosquito and Spitfire photographic aircraft were airborne mainly on bomb damage assessment sorties covering the effect of the previous night's Bomber Command efforts. I had gone up to the Air Traffic Control tower to watch the arrival of at least two American squadrons which had been diverted to Benson. There were over thirty heavy bombers circling the airfield, breaking off in threes from their formations to join the circuit for landing.

Their precision flying was truly remarkable and streams of Fortresses and Liberators appeared nose to tail, out of the mist, on the final approach to the runway. Their pilots took no notice of the Controller's landing instructions from the tower and just pressed on with their usual bad weather landing techniques. Eventually the Controller gave up and let them get on with it – after all, twelve or fifteen of them had already landed safely and all was going well.

A Spitfire joined the melee, made the usual radio calls and attempted to slot himself into the landing approaches of the bombers. Four times the pilot had to go round again, mainly because of the heavy turbulence of the air behind the big aircraft. The controller, becoming worried because of his persistent attempts to land despite the difficulties, called him on the radio, "Bromide 24, Are you short of fuel? Do you want to declare an emergency?" The Belgian pilot, Paul Meunier, replied "No, thank you, I have plenty of petrol. I have no patience!"

# 12. Belinda

FIVE WEEKS BEFORE the war in Europe ended Bunty and I were married. With Bunty teaching in the north of Scotland and me in the south of England coordination was difficult. However, it was arranged that Glasgow would have the honour of staging the event. (It's half way between Aberdeen and Benson, Bunty said.) We had friends there who would make the basic arrangements and April 2nd was chosen as the Great Day – something to do with fools and taxes I believe! Time off was granted at both ends and the game was on.

In spite of a taxi driver who had never driven in Glasgow before – "Sorry, Guv, I was just obliging a friend who owns the taxi" – and a part-time temporary Constable – "I normally do my patrolling in Greenock but I was transferred here yesterday to this area and I'm learning my beat" – we were only 22 minutes late for the ceremony. If it hadn't been for a drunk who was trying to find his way home (at 11 o'clock in the morning) we would have been much later. Although we had almost given up hope of ever finding Mount Vernon Parish Church we asked the 'happy' man where it was. He looked as us if we were drunk ourselves and said, "There it is, right in front of you," and pointed to a spire a couple hundred yards away. We thanked him effusively and I heard him mumble to himself, "Funny folk, they must be drunk".

Bunty must have forgiven me for being late but I didn't think her father, George Mackay, did. He'd been patrolling the street outside checking his watch every 30 seconds. The ceremony was short and so was the reception.

## Memoirs of a High Flyer

Bunty and I took the afternoon train to London. At King's Cross Station Hotel we were given a room with separate beds but economy in everything in wartime had taught us well and we used only one. Next day we went to Symonds Yat on the Welsh border, a really beautiful spot for a honeymoon where we again economised when we found they had given us separate rooms. Bunty must have thought long and hard about the three clangers in the first 36 hours of our married life. Maybe she's still considering what action to take after 60 years.

I bought my first car at Benson. It was an old Austin 7, about as big as a Mini, with two seats in the front and a 'dickey seat' behind. The owner wanted £20 for it. £20 was nearly two weeks' pay in those days but the deciding factor in my purchase was that the petrol tank was over half full. Petrol was severely rationed even in the Services though no doubt some members had improper access to fuel. If your journey wasn't necessary you didn't go. The car had no headlights and suffered from an incurable disease in the steering mechanism. This latter condition soon turned out to be in my favour because the country roads around southern Oxfordshire, all of which seemed to lead to the best pubs, were narrow and not well cambered. I soon got used to Belinda's habit ('Belinda' was Bunty's choice of name for our new possession) of taking a sudden turn, left or right, it didn't seem to matter which, when driving along these narrow roads. Her top speed was not terribly high which was just as well because every time Belinda took a turn (to coin a phrase) in either direction she didn't come to much harm whatever sort of hedge she encountered. I was very satisfied with her because I became aware of a slight tremor through the steering wheel which preceded each of her directional misdemeanours. (It took me that entire half-tank of fuel to discover the tremor but it was worth it.) Whenever any of my colleagues asked to borrow Belinda for a pub run or to impress a girl with his driving prowess I gave him the key (there was only one) and said, "You can take her away provided you put some petrol in the tank. Let me have the key back tomorrow". For some reason I was never asked the same favour again by any of my friends who drove her.

It was perhaps just as well that there was no M.O.T. in those days. I never held a driving licence either because most active serving personnel were expected, I suppose, to be able to move a vehicle from A to B as required. I learned by watching what real drivers did and trying to remember the techniques required to, for example, change gear, when the time came for me to try. Of course there were many fewer mad drivers on the road then. My first trip on acquiring Belinda was, of course, celebratory. So I chose to visit the local hostelry which was at the top of a slight hill, close to the Mess. Four of my colleagues came too. I got the impression that Belinda was not very happy to have five on board, she creaked a bit as they clambered aboard but the engine was full of vitality, especially in the lower gears. We reached the London Road Inn in a very short time in spite of the hill and the fact that, as one of my passengers said, "She'd go better with the handbrake off".

Belinda was necessarily left out every night and I made sure she would not freeze up on cold nights by emptying out the water from the cooling system. I checked with the Met Office one evening in December '44 and they assured me that the temperature wouldn't go below freezing point that night. It did, of course, well below. The next day I opened the bonnet to find all four core plugs standing out of the sides of the engine on stalks of ice. The engine block was cracked to about 1/20th of an inch all the way around. To me, this was the end of a beautiful friendship with the Met Office and the source of tears and bewailing when I contemplated the possibility of repairs. Where could I get a replacement Austin 7 engine in wartime? How could I afford it, anyway? One of my friends suggested fire cement for the engine block crack and halfpenny coins to fill the core plug holes. I tried his recommendations and Belinda never knew anything had happened. She never looked back.

I kept Belinda until I knew I was going to be posted and then I let it be known I was willing to part with a most remarkable vehicle. I had a call from a Roman Catholic padre from a village about 12 miles away showing interest in my offer. I explained fully all of Belinda's shortcomings but he seemed more than keen. I suggested he brought a mechanically minded friend with him to check the car fully and he agreed. I also mentioned that I was looking for a £20 sale price. He came, he saw, he liked, he paid. His motor mechanic friend said there would be a certain amount of work to be done including the engine repairs but £20 was a fair price.

As they drove away I said I would wait by the phone for the next half hour in case he had any problems and I would get one of my mobile friends to come to the rescue. I never heard from him again. However, Bunty said one day that she'd been in Wallingford and she had seen a sparkling new Austin 7 drive past with Belinda's number plate, but it was a pretty blue colour instead of the drab oatmeal we remembered. It is amazing how much effort and expense a loving congregation will go to ensure their religious mentor is properly fitted out with transport. But then, after all, he was a Roman Catholic.

# 13. Flying Without Oxygen

THE AUTHORITIES MUST have been more than satisfied with my airborne activities because on March 20th 1945 I went with my mother to Buckingham Palace where King George VI invested me with the Distinguished Flying Cross (D.F.C.).

Towards the end of the conflict in Europe, rather reminiscent of the end of hostilities in the Mediterranean, the Germans were desperate for the supply of aviation fuel for their tanks and aircraft. The allies were equally desperate to prevent them from producing it. Refineries all over Europe were attacked day and night by the U.S. 8th Air Force and Bomber Command.

A giant oil refinery was located at Magdeburg in northern Germany about 75 miles west of Berlin and was subjected to numerous day and night attacks. The weather was not on our side because a complete cover of low stratus cloud remained static over North-West Europe for long periods, and this prevented our photo reconnaissance squadrons from producing evidence to show whether Magdeburg and other oil targets were irrevocably damaged or still producing. At last it was decided that evidence must be obtained, the best chance being for a Spitfire to carry out the task. However, the Spitfire's only navigational equipment consisted of a compass and a clock, so it was planned that I should fly in close formation with a Mosquito (which had excellent navigational aide) to a chosen spot 25 miles south of the target. At that point, on a signal from the Mosquito pilot, I would break away from the formation and dive at a specified engine setting, airspeed, rate of descent and compass heading until I entered the blanket of cloud. I would then continue descending until I broke cloud below the overcast. It was then up to me to look for the target which should be a mile or two ahead. The aircraft was fitted with a side-facing camera in the fuselage. I would also be expected to provide a visual report on the state of the refinery. My return to base would necessitate my remaining in the low cloud layer.

Clearly, it was necessary to test this plan as soon as possible so I flew in formation with a Benson mosquito. My target from 25,000 ft. was Kings Lynn. The game was on. The technique was evidently workable.

I did not sleep particularly well that night because I was well aware that this flight could be a one-way operation, but, as usual with the young men and women of that time, nothing could happen to me. Nevertheless, I breathed a sigh of relief the next morning when I was told the flight had been cancelled – the blanket of low cloud over the whole area had broken up overnight and that the normal high level photographic coverage of Magdeburg would be possible. I have often wondered what my parents, who lived about 15 miles from Benson, had thought of the particularly fond farewell I had given them when I made a short visit the evening before.

Prior to D-Day landings, aircraft from Benson had carried out sorties at very low level in preparation for the invasion. The Spitfires had been fitted with a camera in the port wing, facing forward. Coverage of the beaches had been required to determine what barriers and obstacles had been sunk into the sand by the Germans to prevent aircraft and gliders from landing and to make seaborne landings by Tank Landing Craft and Infantry Landing Craft extremely difficult.

Most of the Spitfire pilots at Benson were given the opportunity to practise really low flying. This was exhilarating stuff because R.A.F. rules, even in wartime, precluded flight below 250ft. We used railway lines in the Swindon area for this exercise, remembering that every mile or so the telephone and railway signalling wires crossed over the tracks. I also practised low flying when returning from a sortie. I flew along broad stretches of the River Thames where bridges were the only obstacles.

On one such occasion I approached Caversham Bridge a few feet above the water and pulled the aircraft up to fly over it by about 20ft. My mother's butcher-boy was at that moment crossing the bridge carrying the meat rations for that week on a tray. Regrettably, the surprise generated by the passage of an aeroplane just above his head caused him to release his tray and meat was consigned to the depths of Old Father Thames. The local fish no doubt enjoyed the pleasant surprise. I didn't enjoy my reception on my next visit home.

The London Road Inn, located at the top of a slight hill above the Officers' Mess was the favourite haunt of many of the aircrews at Benson. For one thing it was within strolling distance and if the local 'bobby' should happen to appear after eleven any evening he was on our side and was happy to be entertained in the kitchen area until quite late. Earlier on in the war the Inn had caught on fire and many R.A.F. personnel had raced up the hill (of course) to help extinguish the blaze. The pub's owner was most grateful for the help given and when the great day came, D-Day, and many of us retired there to celebrate, he asked our particular group what we planned to do. We said we'd go into Reading and see what was going on there. He said, "Before you go, have a pint or two of the Black Velvet on me. It will form an excellent basis in your system for what is obviously going to be a night of drinking". Champagne and Guinness wasn't my cup of tea but I wasn't caring at that stage. Five of us went to Reading but couldn't get into any of the dances or shindigs which had been hastily arranged so we planned to go back to the Mess as soon as we had had a celebratory drink at my parents' favourite pub, 'The Moderation'. (What a name for a pub!) As we drove off we passed the Reading Fire Station....

The Duty Crew at the Fire Station invited us in to their Operations Room upstairs. When we left, one bright spark asked if we could slide down their pole. "Of course, look, it's easy." So saying, one of the firemen dashed across the room, flung himself at the shiny, slippery pole and disappeared from sight in a flash. Another fireman, who noticed our looks of horror at what seemed to be one of the quickest ways to commit suicide, said, "Of course, you don't need to do it that way, Try this". He walked quietly to the pole, grasped it firmly with one arm and gently disappeared from view, stopping once or twice on the way by tightening his grip. We all followed. I really forget the rest of that evening – I only recall the realisation of a child's dream – To slide down a fireman's pole.

## Memoirs of a High Flyer

Many Squadrons stood down when the hostilities ceased. The P.R. Squadrons, however, took on extra work, mainly of such tasks as photo coverage of large areas for town planning, especially in the U.K. Benson aircraft covered the whole coastline of north-western Europe from Norway to the Spanish border with infra-red film for water-depth studies. Numerous other requirements came up for coverage now that the photography over much of Europe could be undertaken without interruption. The whole of the U.K. was photographed at a particular height with certain focal-length cameras to assist production of up-to-date maps by the Ordinance Survey people.

On one occasion I was given an area of Yorkshire to cover on a perfect day – good light, good visibility, light winds aloft, etc. I planned my flight to make twelve runs, six each way North/South and South/North over the area. The flight there was uneventful and I started to carry out the mosaic task. I was so pleased with the way things went that I finished off the square with an East-West run at both ends to provide a 'perfect' result. I considered that my expertise in this particular performance would be admired and approved by the experts back at Base. On my return, I said I had completed the task and I would like to see the result when the film had been processed. The next morning I was invited to the photo planning section and was asked if I'd like to see the full track of the previous day's flight. Naturally, I expected a measure of approval, even perhaps a modicum of admiration because I knew I'd done a good job. I was mortified when I saw the whole picture. My photo showed that I had started well and the first few runs had gone according to plan but shortly afterwards the track depicted by the photos left Yorkshire altogether, crossed over Lancashire and drifted over the Irish Sea. The film ran out as I crossed Anglesey. My only excuse was that perhaps I had suffered from anoxia due to an oxygen system failure. A check of the oxygen equipment in the aircraft revealed a disconnected union. I had flown without oxygen at 16,000 ft. for long enough to lose all sense of what I was doing or where I was going, yet I was absolutely convinced I was doing very well.

Some of our Spitfires were modified slightly so that Winston Churchill's mail could be taken immediately to him at the Potsdam Conference in Berlin. I was lucky enough to be chosen to do two of these runs to Berlin/Gatow during the Conference period. The plan was to take the mail there each morning, spend the night in the city and return with mail the next morning to Benson. We shared the airspace over Berlin with dozens of heavy transport aeroplanes operating in the 'Berlin airlift' scheme. I was able to go down into Hitler's bunker, a most dismal and depressing place, during my first visit and although it was closely guarded by the Russians no difficulty was experienced in moving around as I wished. I visited the Medal Room which was knee-deep in ribbons. The shelves and racks had been cleared completely but among the medals on the floor I managed to equip myself with an Iron Cross and several items of interest including a medal cast for the Spanish Army Division which had fought on the Russian front. As I wandered through the private quarters of the bunker I came across some beautiful wine and champagne glasses and I brought a dozen away. Some I gave away but I still have one left, after sixty years.

I also took the opportunity to visit various famous buildings and was particularly lucky to see the famous Head of Nefertiti in a museum in what became the Russian Sector of Berlin. The city was in a terrible mess, and although the main streets had been cleared and a few trams were running, the side streets were piled with rubble. It seemed strange to be able to fly low over Berlin and other cities which I had visited up high on photographic missions such a short time before.

Not long after my to visits to Berlin I was asked to ferry a P.R. Spitfire XIX to the Far East in company with another Squadron pilot. I jumped at the opportunity because flying mosaics every time over U.K and the Continent was becoming repetitive. No-one could resist this wonderful offer.

My colleague and I took off and flew by the way of Portreath in Cornwall, Bordeaux, Marseille, Rome, Malta, Castel Benito in Tripoli and El Adem to Cairo. We were delayed three weeks in Cairo for a replacement Griffon engine to be flown out from the UK. The policy was for the two aircraft to stay together for safety reasons so I was required to wait until both were serviceable. I didn't mind, of course, a holiday in Egypt for three weeks – if only Bunty could have joined me! Anyway, there was no spare money available so we had a fairly quiet time. One advantage we had was being billeted in Shepheard's Hotel.

**Memoirs of a High Flyer**

We left Cairo and flew to Habbaniyah, Bahrain, Karachi, Jodhpur, Allahabad, and finally, through some heavy monsoon weather, to Calcutta. Unfortunately, that was the end of my Far East escapade because two squadron pilots were already champing at the bit waiting for us to arrive. We watched them disappear to the East as soon as they refuelled. A day or two in Calcutta was quite enough and we were Dakota-borne back to the UK.

This formal portrait was taken around 1942/43, Keith would have been a Flight Lieutenant by this point as can be seen from the two stripes on his right shoulder.

Formal portrait of Bunty taken in 1942/43.

 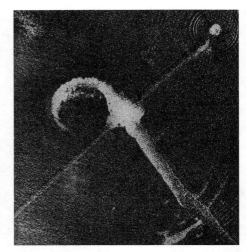

**Above left:** A photograph taken of Keith in Cairo during his stay there in 1945.

**Above right:** A unique photograph taken by Keith of an enemy aircraft that dropped a bomb close to where a submarine was.

**Below:** Keith with Sheila and Christopher.

This photograph of the American Ford was taken in Sumter, South
Carolina, with a young Sheila in the driving seat, 1950.

A Ponca City reunion in October 1991. The plane pictured is the same one
Keith learned to fly in 50 years previously.
Keith stood on the right, happy to be back in Oklahoma.

This family photograph was taken in 1982 in Nairn. From left to right: Nonny, Keith, Esme (held by Keith), Aunty Mona, Sheila, Bunty. Front row: Mark, Davina.

Keith succeeding in fitting into a slightly smaller car than usual, taken at Sheila's house in Greece,1986.

Christmas 1986, sledging with granddaughter Davina.

Like father, like son. Son Christopher also enjoying the thrills of flying, taken in Cyprus, 1994. A notable photograph as Christopher is the instructor and Keith the pupil!

A selection of photographs from
Keith and Bunty's 50th wedding
anniversary, April 1995.

Family Christmas 1997 in Oxford.

Bunty and Keith during a woodlands walk in Perthshire, 1997/98.

Bunty and Keith photographed at a 'Scottish night' in 1998. The back of the photo has a message in Bunty's handwriting, "I'm sure we each had a drink and didn't have to share".

This picture of Bunty, Keith and Sheila was taken in a chalet in Dalfaber, 2009.

Granddaughter Esme modelling a t-shirt with the words, "My Grandad Flew Spitfires". Taken in Greece, 1984.

# AFTER THE WAR

# 14. Wrong Bloody Tuesday

LIKE MOST OTHER Volunteer Reserve Officers in the Air Force, it was time to consider future prospects most carefully, especially now that Bunty and I were married. My original idea of becoming a teacher had floundered. The thrill of flying had me in its grip and I did not want it to release its hold. Bunty joined me when her 1944-45 teaching year was over and because she enjoyed great satisfaction from her fine teaching skills we decided that if the R.A.F. would provide me with a permanent commission she could offer her services as a supply teacher wherever we were sent. This decision has resulted in some really wonderful experiences for both of us in the UK, USA, Germany and Africa.

Accordingly, I applied to the Air Force for a permanent commission and settled myself down to study the history of the R.A.F. and two of the most disagreeable subjects that anyone could dream up – Air Force Law and King's Regulations & Air Council Instructions. I must have chosen the correct course of action because after a couple of exams and a gruelling week's session on an officer's training course, I was accepted 'into the body of the kirk'.

In July 1946, I was posted to the Central Flying School (CFS) at R.A.F. Little Rissington in Gloucestershire. CFS is the school for instructors in the Royal Air Force. CFS examiners visit R.A.F. stations all over the world to ensure that proper training standards are maintained. Many of the countries who had been our allies during the war would send their pilots for instructor training to CFS and would adopt its training techniques for their own air forces.

At first, Bunty and I stayed in bed and breakfast accommodation next to the church in Bourton-on-the-Water. Each morning we were wakened by a verse of a hymn, played on the church bells – much better than nowadays when one wakes to the sound of police sirens. Bourton is a particularly attractive village with a stream running right down the centre. It also boasts a reproduction of itself in miniature, faithfully portrayed, and even a miniature version of the miniature itself.

The course at CFS was scheduled to last about four months so we searched for more permanent digs in the local area. This we found in the village of Bledington where we took two furnished rooms in a farmhouse. Next to our bedroom was the most modern and ornate bathroom we'd ever seen, with gold taps and other fittings of the very latest design. Sadly, there was no water laid on and the original 'shed down the bottom of the garden' was still in use. Our living room downstairs was cosy but it was lit and heated by paraffin lamps and heaters. However, the cattle were housed in three sheds which formed a square with the farmhouse. The midden was, of course, in the middle of the square. Electric lighting and heating were available for the cattle in each shed. In other words a typical English farm set up.

The farmer, a most pleasant old man, was not permitted by his wife to smoke his pipe in the house so he wandered around the midden whenever he wanted a puff. Once each fortnight, on a Tuesday, an itinerant cinema operator came to the village hall with a film show and our farmer friend would get dressed in his Sunday best clothes and would spend the evening in the arms of Hollywood. One day we saw him pass by the window, hall-bound, properly dressed, but we were surprised to see him returning some ten minutes later, looking very out-of-sorts. "Wrong bloody Tuesday", he growled as he went by.

Bunty took on a teaching job at nearby Kingham, a cycle ride away, during our stay at CFS. The school provided lunch for all the children and staff, the cook suggested that since blackberries (or brambles for Scots readers) were plentiful that year, the Headmaster might like to ask the children to pick some for a pie. He agreed, but went a bit overboard and said, "For every pound you collect, boys and girls, I'll give you twopence". One hundred and fifty pounds later he begged them to stop. We had blackberries in every form known to the cooking fraternity. I still love bramble and apple pie but, after all, there was a limit.

I had joined No. 94 course at CFS in July 1946 and I found it tough going. However, after eighty-odd hours of flying under instruction and of flights in company with another student where we were required to practise set exercises, talking each manoeuvre through as if the other was a trainee (these were called 'mutual exercises'). I achieved a satisfactory standard and was issued with a 'B' Instructor's License.

One of the students with whom I did 'mutuals' with was Ray Lygo who, later, was knighted and became Chief of the Naval Staff. Another was Prince Antoine De Ligne, a Belgian ex-fighter pilot and what he didn't know about aerobatic manoeuvres and instruments wasn't worth knowing. One day we were sent aloft to do mutual aerobatic exercises. I suggested I should do the instructor bit first and he could judge my efforts and after twenty minutes or so he could take control and do his turn. He agreed, so I climbed up through the overcast which had about 1,000 feet base and tops about 2,000 feet and broke out into beautiful sunshine. I completed a series of standard aerobatic exercises with the required 'patter' and then handed over to Antoine. He certainly knew his stuff. He immediately turned the Harvard upside down, pulled the stick back and dove into the cloud below. We spent the next fifteen minutes doing aerobatics in the cloud with this 'maniac' talking away at me as if I were his pupil.

Every now and then, for a fleeting second, I saw either the sunshine at the top of a loop or the gloomy ground below at the bottom of some manoeuvre or other. In the last few minutes we zoomed below cloud and I just had time to spot something on the ground that I recognised.

Back into cloud again and Antoine said, "O.K., I've done my lot, let's get back to base".

I said, "Right, steer 240 degrees and start letting down on that heading".

After a short interval I said, "O.K, now turn left on to 150 and do your vital actions for landing".

For some reason, better known to him, he did as I suggested, seeming to have some trust in what I said.

"Right, now continue your descent and call Air Traffic and tell them we're

89

downwind high." He did so and we were given permission to land, no other traffic being in the area.

I said, "O.K., turn left on to 060 degrees and after ten seconds on that heading turn left again onto 330. When we break cloud you'll see the runway ahead".

All went well and we landed from that approach. I had, and still have to this day, an enormous respect for his aerobatic ability. I still have the impression that he looked with disbelief on my ability to navigate an aircraft for an hour, doing aerobatics above and in cloud and still get exactly onto the final approach for landing without any guidance whatsoever. Little did he know (and I didn't tell him) that on our final dip below the cloud I had seen the letters LR in white on the ground in the signals square beside Air Traffic Control at our base at Little Rissington.

My next posting, my first as a fully-fledged instructor, was to R.A.F. Ouston, near Newcastle and situated very close to Hadrian's Wall amid wide open countryside. Here, the R.A.F. instructors were teaching Naval Officers the advanced stage to Wings standard. Once again, the faithful, noisy Harvard was our tool. The successful trainees would then to go the RN Base at Arbroath to learn the specialised deck-landing techniques on land in preparation for the real thing on an aircraft carrier.

Shortly after my arrival at Ouston the Navy invited a few of the instructors to spend a week on the Vengeance, a training aircraft carrier, to see how the last course of students were progressing. They had finished at Arbroath, had converted to Seafires (a naval version of the Spitfire with a strengthened undercarriage and an arrester hook fitted below the fuselage) and were now to experience the real test – landing on a deck that is made of steel and is heaving up and down. They were under the control of experienced 'batsmen' whose task it was to get them to a point where they were about to touch down a few yards before their arrester hook would catch a steel wire stretched access the deck, if the aircraft's approach was unsatisfactory, they were waved off to go around for another try. An emergency steel net was located half-way along the deck to catch any aircraft that escaped the precautions taken to stop them. It was a fascinating week. The new pilots each did at least twelve landing and not one Seafire was damaged. The sea air no doubt did me a power of good, and life aboard the Vengeance was full of surprises and it was intensely interesting to a landlubber like me.

# 15. Jane

BUNTY WAS BY NOW expecting our first child but decided to do some teaching for a few months in 1947. Sheila Morne was born in May of that year in a nursing home which also cared for 'battle-damaged' footballers. I got the distinct impression that the nursing home staff were far more interested in the repair of damaged sinews and legs of these virile young men than the arrival of a miniature specimen of the human race. And what a specimen she turned out to be!

At this time the weather had been particularly bad – one of the coldest that could be remembered by the locals – the winter lasted until late April in the north, it wasn't until then that the snow began to disappear. Conditions were so bad that, although we'd been able to find a small cottage near Ponteland, we couldn't move into it for many weeks, the roads were impassable. Rationing was still making life difficult and shortage of commodities not still on ration didn't help.

I had found another second-hand car. This was Jane, an upright, vintage Standard and although she was a step up in the motoring world after Belinda, there were nevertheless difficulties to be overcome. For instance Jane's starter-motor wouldn't work. It was quite kaput and there was no hope of getting a replacement. I did have a detachable starting handle but I lost it one day in deep snow, from them on I had to rely for starting her on a nearby steep hill, running down fast enough to do a clutch start. The other problems were minor, like poor brakes and no windscreen wiper motor. However, I reduced the effect of the first by very early braking at the first sign of a problem ahead. Bunty fixed up a clever system of cords and coordination whereby, if it rained or snowed too hard to ignore, we opened our side windows and, with the cords attached to the wiper arms, she pulled to and fro with gusto and with "a short uneasy motion" (Coleridge). With all her shortcomings Jane was still a 'duchess of the road', with her deep-stroke engine, her proud, upright stance, her leather-bound interior and her very comfortable ride.

The cottage we had rented turned out to be very cosy, ideal for a new-born baby and her parents. It had been the gatehouse guarding a long drive over a hill to a large house. There was a tennis court sized earthen courtyard beside the cottage and in my enthusiasm to make use of my spare time I decided to plant vegetables over the area.

"Plant potatoes first to clear the ground," said my expert colleagues. So I did. First of all I needed to dig over the ground. My first downward thrust produced a ringing sound from the spade and a strong jolt to my arm. I found that about four inches of soil had been covering a cobbled yard. The cobblestones averaged four inches diameter, ideal for cannonballs. Having been determined to dig for victory, I carried on only to find that the stones had been set out on a heavy bed of clay – that had to be dug through too.

Fortunately, I had plenty of energy. Unfortunately, I had very little knowledge of agricultural matters. In the shed beside the cottage I found a dibber made obviously from a spade handle. It was a little less than two feet long. Naturally, I assumed that 2ft was about the depth you planted potatoes. Well, you would, wouldn't you? I planted Maris Piper across the whole area and sat back and waited. August and September came – not a sign of anything growing but weeds. Everyone else was producing beautiful new spuds. Eventually, at Christmas, there was evidence of some activity. In February/March we had the most marvellous crop of new potatoes, all our own work, when everybody else had to make do with 'last year's crop'. Only one snag – I had to dig down two feet to get them.

Sheila made excellent progress and every Sunday morning I took her out in her pram – the proud father bit. One Sunday when she was a few months old I passed by a house where a young man was digging the garden and looking after a small baby in a pram. This child was yelling his head off, in obvious discomfort. I stopped to pass the time of day with the man.

The chat got round, as it always does, to the relative merits of the offspring. Sheila was quiet, gurgling gently to herself and taking no notice of the screaming child. I, the knowledgeable father, suggested that diet was often the cause of such reactions as screaming all the time.

He said, "We don't really know why he does this, he gets the same as we do, I can't understand it".

I asked what they'd fed the infant that morning.

He said, "He had the same as we did. Sunday is always kippers, tea, toast and marmalade. Always has been. I can't understand it".

When the commitment for training naval personnel at Ouston came to an end I was moved to No. 3 FTS at R.A.F. Feltwell in Norfolk, a grass airfield and one of Flying Training Command's oldest units. Bunty and I found accommodation in the village nearby in a very pleasant old building which, from its appearance, was appropriately named 'The Cottage'. Our landlady, a keen gardener – her asparagus tasted wonderful – immediately fell in love with Sheila. The Grand National was due to be run and a prominent entry that year was 'Sheila's Cottage'. The landlady put a hefty bet on it; we did our usual 'five bob each way'. When Sheila's Cottage romped home we all had good reason to celebrate.

Feltwell had been the 'guinea pig station' chosen to try out a different scheme of flying training, whereby instead of training new students at one station on elementary aircraft and then transferring them to fly advanced aircraft at another station, the trainee would be kept at one unit throughout, using the two types of aircraft at the same station. The advantages of this scheme were not relevant to this account of my experience but it meant that I would be training two students in basic flying on Tiger Moths and two on advanced flying on Harvards.

I arrived at R.A.F. Feltwell on a Friday afternoon and reported to the Chief Flying Instructor. He said I would start on Monday morning with two students who were about half way through the basic course and two more just starting on Harvards. I told him that I had never flown Tigers and I'd like a little time to get the hang of the aircraft. He said, "No problem, I'll arrange a Tiger for you tomorrow morning to use the whole weekend. That way you can get to know the local area so you won't get lost, and get used to the feel of the Tiger, the speeds, power settings etc. that you'll need to establish".

**Memoirs of a High Flyer**

The next two days I spent aloft doing all the things I thought I needed to do to convince my students that I knew what I was doing and that they were in good hands. Monday dawned and I met my two Tiger Moth students. I asked them what stage they had reached in their training so far. Apparently they had just started aerobatics; they had just done loops, slow rolls and barrel rolls. I briefed them on the morning flight and got airborne with Cadet South. We did a few loops and having corrected the odd error I spoke to him through the Gosport tube, the only means of communication between the two cockpits, and said, "That's fine South, now let's have a look at your slow rolls. You do one for me and we'll see how you get on".

He put the Tiger into a slight dive to build up speed then raised the nose above the horizon. He started the rolling manoeuvre and got the aircraft onto its back in a smooth but slow manner. When we were inverted the engine stopped. I had not expected this but there we were, upside down, nose high, speed falling off rapidly and the propeller looking very solid and immoveable. I picked up the speaking tube and said, "South, did your previous instructor show you what to do if your engine stops?" He said, "Yes sir". So I said, "Well, what are you waiting for? Get on with it".
He pulled the nose down into the inverted position, moved the stick back until we were in a vertical dive. The speed built up rapidly. At about 120 knots he applied a short jerk to the elevator and, sure enough, the engine restarted. Fuel from the overhead tank between the wings had ceased to flow while we were inverted but all was well now. I learned something that day from my student about the Tiger Moth which I should have found out for myself the previous weekend.

In mid-1948 I grabbed an opportunity to transfer from Flying Training Command to Fighter Command where there was a vacancy for a Spitfire-qualified QFI at Chivenor in North Devon. Life as an instructor in Flying Training Command was definitely not an appealing future for me, as can be appreciated in this light-hearted poem –

What did you do in the war, Daddy?
How did you help us to win?
Circuits and bumps and turns, laddy,
And how to get out of a spin.

Woe and alack and misery me!
I trundle around in the sky,
And instead of machine gunning Nazis
I'm teaching young hopefuls to fly.

Thus is my service rewarded,
My years of experience paid,
Never a Hun have I followed
Nor ever gone out on a raid.

They don't even let us go crazy,
We have to be safe and sedate,
So it's nix on inverted approaches,
They stir up the C.F.I's hate!

For it's oh such a naughty example,
And what will the A.O.C think!
But we never get posted to fighters,
We just get a spell on the link.

So it's circuits and bumps from morning till noon,
And instruments flying till tea.
Hold her off, give her bank, put your undercart down,
You're skidding; you're skipping that's me.

**Memoirs of a High Flyer**

As soon as soon as you've finished with one course
Like a flash up another bobs,
And there's four more to show round the cockpit
And four more to try out the knobs.

But sometimes we read in the papers
Of the deeds that old pupils have done,
And we're proud to have seen their beginnings
And shown them the way to the sun.

So if you find the money, and turn out the planes
We'll give all we know to the men
Till they cluster the sky with their triumphs
And burn out the Beast from his den.

What did you do in the war, Daddy?
How did you help us to win?
Circuits and bumps and turns, laddy,
And how to get out of a spin.

'The Flying Instructor's Lament' by Pilot Officer O.C. Chave (1940).

# 16. Mark Twain Country

AS USUAL, I went ahead to this new station to look for digs and get them organised. Poor Bunty's task was to follow on in due course with Sheila and all our worldly goods, on her own if necessary.

I arrived at Chivenor railway station at about 4:00pm and an R.A.F. car was waiting. It was a Saturday and the Officers' Mess was silent and deserted (most non-operational R.A.F. stations are very quiet at weekends) except for a lone figure who was nursing a beer in the bar and was, I was sure, almost crying into it. He looked up when he saw me walk in.

"Are you Flight Lieutenant Durbidge by any chance?" I admitted the fact. He said, "Thank God. You're Duty Officer this weekend. Here are the keys and the duty roster. Cheerio".

He departed with alacrity and a huge smile on his face. He even left his beer. I had often been in full charge of an R.A.F. station before as Duty Officer but never without the slightest knowledge of where anything was located. Fortunately the Guardroom staff were efficiently run; a car and driver were available if needed and no earth-shaking emergencies occurred that weekend.

Our stay at Chivenor was fairly short but it was wonderful to get my hands on a Spitfire again. The unit's task was comparatively simple, using Harvards for check flights and Spitfires for formation practice. The students were all experienced pilots converting to Spitfires for Fighter Command.

We found accommodation in Barnstaple with two elderly and delightful ladies who adored Sheila on sight, even after she had ruined a whole wall in the newly decorated dining room. Sitting at breakfast in her highchair she suddenly said, "NO!" and threw her hands up over her head, seemingly unaware that her chubby fingers were still firmly gripping her mug of milk. We must have been forgiven because we kept in touch with the two ladies for the next 40-50 years until their demise. When we drove from Feltwell to Chivenor all our worldly goods would fit into Jane. We were hoarding sugar at the time and kept every spare teaspoonful in a four-pound tin which had held Sheila's milk powder. This tin was strapped on to a metal grid which jutted out, if required, behind Jane's rear end. As we passed through a village near Oxford, a bump in the road dislodged the tin, along with other items, with a loud rattle. The noise disturbed a man digging in his garden. He came over to help collect the items strewn along the road. There was no remedy but to use a rope to tie things down. He went back to his house saying he had the very thing and returned with an ideal solution. We thanked him and offered to return his rope in due course (a valuable commodity in those hard days). He said, "No, that's alright, the wife won't miss her clothes line for ages. I'll maybe get her a new one".

Barnstaple was a pleasant town in excellent surroundings and near the sea but it had one real shortcoming. The town's electrical supply was on Direct Current instead of Alternating Current and it meant that a convertor was needed to run ancillary equipment. Our new table-top record player needed a converter the size of a cabin trunk and it weighed a ton. How things have changed! Nowadays, music centres are as big as cabin trunks and all they need is a cable to a power plug.

We had settled in quite happily in North Devon and were enjoying a very warm 'summer by the sea'; we had even begun to understand the language. However, the authorities had other ideas. The Air Ministry sent out a signal to all likely units offering a one-year posting on exchange duties with the United States Air Force. The requirement was, ideally, for a commissioned Spitfire pilot, in current flying practice, with photo reconnaissance experience, preferably married with family and also preferably decorated and free of personal or R.A.F. commitments. I had all the required qualifications and replied to the signal immediately. My application was successful and by the end of the year I was on my way once again on a voyage to America. Poor

Bunty, another move, another change of plans, and another return to Nairn with Sheila. She was able to look forward to a year free of rationing, free of austerity and shortages, a land flowing with milk and honey and speaking the same tongue. Foreign travel for the first time also afforded some excitement.

In December 1948, I boarded the Mauritania and found another R.A.F. officer sharing a cabin with me. He was also starting an exchange tour with the USAF as a fighter representative. I recall waking up one night to find him fast asleep although the cabin seemed to be standing on its end. I could not resist going out on deck to see what was turning the world upside down. The Mauritania was built in the shape of a deep 'V' which tended to prevent it from rolling in heavy seas. A typical Atlantic storm had developed with enormously high waves speeding towards the ship. The captain had obviously decided to steer straight at them, slicing through like a knife and this resulted in a plunging passage through the storm with the ship tilted at an angle of about 30 or 40 degrees to the vertical. I stood on the port side of the deck which now sloped up towards the sky, an unforgettable sight. Arrival in New York, a briefing at the British Military Mission in Washington D.C., and a swift train journey to Fayetteville in North Carolina went like a flash.

My new station was Pope Field, a USAF base shared by No. 161 squadron of the 10th Tactical Reconnaissance Group and a unit training paratroopers who seemed to loop nonchalantly from C.19 transport aircraft called Boxcars. I was on the base one day when a Boxcar took off and at 60 feet above the ground encountered a large flock of birds which had been frightened by the aircraft's approach. Both engines failed when the birds blocked up the air intakes (can't blame the birds – an approaching Boxcar would scare anybody). The jumpmaster must have been a wonderful influence on his men and he had a thoroughly effective training technique, because even at that perilously low height he got 28 of his 30 trainees out through the open doors in the rear of the Boxcar as the pilot tried to make the best of a crash landing. The last two paratroopers were injured but survived. The jumpmaster then went forward to the cabin and assisted the escape of the pilot and navigator, both also injured, from the wreckage. He was awarded a medal for his bravery and skill, an honour richly deserved.

My arrival at Pope Field gave me an immediate reminder of one of the many idiosyncrasies of military establishments worldwide. On presenting myself at the Guardroom I heard the Sergeant of the Guard say, "Good afternoon. Sir, would you please give me your number, rank and name, and your MOS". I was able to oblige him with the first three items but I was stumped by the fourth. I said, "What do you mean, Sergeant, by MOS?" He said, "Everyone has an MOS and I need to know yours". "Yes, but what is a MOS?" He said, "Why, a Military Occupational Speciality, of course, Sir".

It took me a short while before I could work out the crazy official-ese of MOS. "Pilot, Sergeant," I said. We got quite friendly eventually as he told me how to get to the Officers' Mess and living quarters.

I had been about a fortnight at Fayetteville and was walking back to the airfield one afternoon when a car drew up beside me. The driver said, "I guess you are the British officer who has recently joined us at Pope?" I admitted the fact. "Then climb aboard and we'll have some real English tea." It turned out that Warren Hawes had been with the American forces in Britain during the war and had met and married a London girl. He introduced his attractive wife, Joyce, and that was the start of a long and happy friendship. As luck would have it, Warren and Joyce followed us back to Europe and were posted to Germany at the same time as we were. He had a gentle, almost British, sense of humour and we had many good times together. He 'checked me out' in flying the Dakota and provided me with many opportunities to get accustomed to this sturdy 'warhorse of the air' during a period of comparative quiet when our squadron was changing aircraft types and locations.

When in April 1949 Warren offered me the chance to be 'checked out' on the Dakota I jumped at the opportunity. He was required to take about twenty US Army soldiers to Craig Field in Alabama for an exercise. We took off with me following closely the checks and procedures and noting the engine power settings, temperatures, pressures and all the usual requirements for a normal flight. I flew the aircraft most of the way and Warren said, "You're doing fine, why don't you do the landing". All was well until we were a few feet off the ground and I was holding the aircraft off in the approved manner for a three-point landing. Warren suddenly turned towards me, grabbed my left arm firmly and said, "Keith, have you paid your income tax this year yet?" After what must have been the bounciest landing that poor Dakota had ever made I managed to taxi it to the control tower unaided. As Warren walked down the central aisle to the rear exit he said to the soldiers, "He did the landing, not me". That was the roughest 'conversion-to-type' I made throughout my career. I did forgive him, however – after all, he signed my logbook to the effect that I was competent on the type. Joyce and Warren and their three children spent many very happy hours with Bunty and Sheila when the latter arrived that Spring.

No. 161 squadron were using the reconnaissance version of the Mustang fighter aircraft. This aircraft had made such a difference towards the end of the war due to its ability, when fitted with the Rolls Royce Merlin engine, to equal the Me 109 in performance when escorting Fortresses and Liberators on their long-range daylight bombing raids into Germany. I considered the Mustang to be a very suitable vehicle for the reconnaissance task as it was dependable, nearly as easy to handle as the Spitfire, and a very stable camera platform. I managed to get nearly fifty hours experience on the Mustang before the squadron converted to jet aircraft. During this period of change we moved to Langley Field in Virginia to carry out pilot training on the RF 80, the reconnaissance version of the F 80, the Shooting Star.

I had not been working with the Americans very long before I realised that a car was an essential 'bit of kit'. Almost all married officers lived off base and the unmarried ones lived in Bachelor Officers' Quarters (BOQs). I had found a small but suitable house in Fayetteville shortly after arrival in the US and applied for Bunty and Sheila to join me. At the same time I wrote to the Air Ministry saying that I found it would be quite impossible on my salary to achieve a standard of living which was clearly required of a Royal Air Force officer. I stated I would need to draw cash from my private account in the UK to finance a suitable standard. I knew that the UK Government was very reluctant to buy US dollars so soon after the end of the war and with austerity still ruling the roost. However, someone in the Air Ministry must have put up a good case on my behalf because just before Bunty and Sheila arrived, I received permission to draw £300 in US dollars (my total worldly wealth) from my UK bank account. I was determined to use the whole amount, if necessary, on a good but second-hand car as soon as I could find one. A week or so after getting the finances arranged I went to New York to meet Bunty and Sheila off the Queen Elizabeth. They had had a memorable voyage with Bunty constantly chasing Sheila as she climbed every step or stairway she could find anywhere on board. I met an exhausted wife and a high-spirited 1 ½ year old off the ship but after a restful night in the Governor Clinton Hotel in New York, we took a train to Washington DC. Here, luck was definitely on our side because in the first car showroom we entered, the salesman, agreed to sell us a Ford 'Forty-Niner' which had been a demonstration car for prospective buyers. It was in excellent condition, of course, and had less than four hundred miles on the clock. We got it for $1200 as, fortunately for us, the US dollar was at that time rated at four to the pound sterling. This big car was perfect for our needs and not a gas guzzler on long journeys. It had a V-8 engine and at 63,000 miles, I felt perhaps I should change the plugs. We drove to Fayetteville in style and great comfort.

Our stay in North Carolina did not last very long and we were soon on our way to Langley Field, Virginia. Bunty and I were quite accustomed to moving to a new station in the R.A.F. Now it seemed easy to make these moves in the US especially as we had a commodious car for all our worldly possessions. The only snag was always having to look for furnished accommodation and, of course, pay the price. We were lucky this time. A small, cosy, comfortable, detached house on a short lease was available, located a few yards from a creek off Chesapeake Bay. Nearby was a small-holding belonging to a Mr and Mrs Clark, a revelation to Bunty and me. He farmed pigs and poultry. These were a source of utter fascination to Sheila. The Clarks, equally, though they had a numerous family, found Sheila completely fascinating and marvelled at her ability to talk clearly and to pick up Americanisms. Mrs Clark was a homely woman, typically American, but her husband seemed to me to be a misfit. He looked and acted like a true Hollywood hobo. Unkempt, rough-spoken, he had the traditional heart of gold. He frequently urged us to have a ride on his horse and one day I was fool enough to accept. In minutes he was back with the biggest creature one could imagine as a horse. I did actually ride it, bareback of course but there was nothing to hold on to. Fortunately, he had a long mane which I grasped tightly and he seemed to realise that I was petrified, so apart from a gallop at about 60 mph and huge jumps over a few low hedges, he treated me kindly. Bunty was sensible enough to agree to sit on the horse and be photographed which is what I should have done. From that moment, I vowed that if offered a ride on a horse I would decline if the creature was bigger than me. We heard later when we moved to South Carolina that they had named their next son Keith. I felt greatly honoured.

In South Carolina I was billeted in the BOQ at Shaw Field for a short while before I was able to find somewhere suitable to let Bunty and Sheila join me. In the BOQ all meals were served cafeteria style. A 'chow-line' was formed in the dining hall and once you were served you carried your tray to wherever you chose to sit. The first Saturday morning I came down to breakfast and found myself behind a Lt. Elmer Barnes, from Texas, one of our squadron members, a young, healthy, hungry country boy. At the serving counter he asked for three large pancakes with molasses while he helped himself to cornflakes and milk. Then, at the 'hot' end he took six eggs with bacon and a huge cup of coffee. I followed him, in awe of his appetite, having requested my slice of toast and marmalade, one egg, bacon and coffee. I sat beside Elmer, talking of various squadron matters and deliberately avoiding speaking of calories and stomach-ache. The next morning, by chance, I was again right behind Elmer in the chow-line. He ordered an exactly similar meal except for seven eggs instead of six. I could not resist asking him why the extra egg? He said, "It's Sunday, you know – Sundays I get a treat".

Elmer was a delightful character – he wore spurs on his flying boots until told to remove them as they were damaging the cockpit floors. In the evenings he spent most of his time playing hill-billy music on his guitar in company with Roy White, another squadron member, who played his one-string fiddle, both singing away mournfully whenever a tear-jerkin' melody was chosen.

The excellent American custom of offering full training for chosen civilian trades to those who served as volunteers was very welcome to Elmer. His father owned a large fenced-in cattle ranch in Texas and employed a large staff of 'cowboys' whose tasks included ensuring the fence was secure. Elmer chose to take a helicopter pilot course so that his love of flying could be carried on 'riding the range' round the fences.

Bunty and I had been able to find very suitable accommodation in Sumter which served out our time in America. We shared the home of a Miss Rembert, a middle-aged lady who had been a missionary in Korea. With a name like hers she was, of course, of Scottish descent and she took very kindly to the three of us, as we did to her. The long, low bungalow was divided down the centre and our five rooms fed into one another quite easily since there was no corridor. It was of wooden construction throughout and all the windows were supplied with metal mosquito netting. These were normally left stacked up beside the house but could be fitted quite quickly if bad weather was expected. Miss Rembert had an elderly servant who was utterly devoted to her and had been a 'plantation slave' to her family during her early life. His skill in fitting the windows all around the house in less than ten minutes was demonstrated one day after we had settled in there. When I arrived at the Squadron Operations Room, the place was jumping. A tornado was forecast and the USAF had decided to evacuate all the precious aircraft to safe havens in Alabama and Georgia. I just had time to dash home, warn Bunty and Miss Rembert of the impending storm and grab some overnight gear. No consideration, you notice, of how wives and families would cope – the safety of the aircraft was paramount. All our planes were bound for Dobbins AF base in Georgia where we spent two lazy days watching reports of the tornado as it disappeared to the north-west, avoiding all the east coast states.

By the time we had spent nearly a year in America, Bunty and I were dreading the official letter from the Air Ministry which would end our one-year tour with the USAF and give us returning instructions to the UK. We had thoroughly enjoyed our stay and had been lucky enough to see a sizeable portion of the north-east of the States. The letter came, containing very apologetic terms, (most unusual for a services letter) not saying, "Your time is up, return to UK as stated below" but, "We sincerely regret that your return to the UK and your loved ones will be delayed for up to a year owing to a complete blockage of accommodation on board both the Queen Mary and Queen Elizabeth for the foreseeable future. This is due to the great number of Americans who have already booked to visit London for the South Bank Exhibition. We trust that you will understand the importance of the influx of millions of dollars to the UK's economy especially at this time of austerity. We also trust that you will accept this change of plan in a true spirit and continue your service with the US Air Force who have already stated their pleasure at this new set of circumstances". My reply said that, naturally, Bunty and I were deeply upset at the change of plan but that we would cooperate to the best of our ability. DRINKS ALL ROUND. This meant that we could make plans for a three week leave of absence which was due to us. A trip across America to the west coast was now possible and there were no travel problems involved.

So we set off on a tour which would take us to San Francisco, Los Angeles and back again to the east coast via Ponca City. We were happy to see Mark Twain country around Hannibal in Missouri; the wonderfully located city of Denver, 5,000 feet up among the Rocky Mountains; and the terraced street system of San Francisco. We crossed the Golden Gate Bridge to marvel at the Muir Woods with its incredible sequoia trees. We took the coast road to Los Angeles in preference to the high speed Pacific Highway and paddled in the Pacific Ocean near Santa Monica. A quick visit to LA and we then turned eastwards speculating at the long, dead-straight ribbon of concrete which crossed the Mojave Desert. We were overtaken by a Greyhound bus on this stretch of highway and we were doing 80 mph. Five miles on, the bus driver waved gaily to us from a roadside courtesy stop where his passengers were slaking their thirst and attending to the wants of nature. We stopped one night near Ely, Nevada, and saw the world's largest copper mine, five miles rim to rim and so deep that the great digger and haulage machines looked like ants. Sheila was getting tired so we stopped at the first hotel we saw. No food there but we were assured the local bar would look after us. The place was empty but for two grizzled old men playing dice at the long bar. Each had a pile of dollars beside him and as one lost a game he paid for more whiskey from his pile. When we came down for breakfast the next morning they were still playing, the pile of dollars much depleted. The barman told us they were gold prospectors who came every eight or nine weeks to spend what cash was left over after they'd paid for their provisions for the next trip. They'd been doing this for years. They panned a river about thirty miles away and had a mule for transport. They always used this particular bar because they were never disturbed!

Our route back east took us past some of the wonders of the west; Hoover Dam, the Petrified Forest; and the Painted Desert. We also called in at Ponca City in Oklahoma where we renewed acquaintanceship with Jock Sturrock, an ex-member of my old squadron at Benson. He had married a Ponca City girl and settled in the States.

# 17. The Higher Authority

THE RF 80 SHOOTING STAR was, like the Mustang, a very stable camera platform and a pleasure to fly but it was very under-powered with the single Allison J-33 jet engine. Our rate of climb was dismal, but with its sturdy build and heavy all-up weight it would build up an acceptable speed at level flight at high altitude if you left the power fully on for a minute or so. The 'solid' nature of the aircraft was clearly demonstrated on a flight I made with a Lt. Jerry Monaghan from base to an area in Florida where we each had large districts to photograph. The outward journey, during which I witnessed a delightful example of serenity and pleasure at 30,000 feet, was uneventful. Jerry was well-known for his appetite and for his love of masses of salad cream on his sandwiches. I led on the outward journey and Jerry was wide on my right wing. As I took a glance at him I saw him with a gaze of pure joy on his face, munching on a large sandwich, no doubt smothered with salad cream. A big smile and a gay wave assured me he was well in control.

On the return flight with Jerry leading we saw a large line squall ahead. Clearly we'd be unable with the power available to climb over it so it meant entering at a steady level and getting through it as quickly as possible. The embedded thunderstorms were fierce and well developed and contained hailstones the size of walnuts. On our return to Shaw Field it transpired that both aircraft would need to have new wings – the many indentations were at least an inch deep into the leading edges. Much worse to come – the RF 80 had a two-inch thick strengthened glass window in the nose to protect the forward-facing camera. The nose window in my aircraft was broken and

107

the camera damaged by the hailstone strikes. Jerry's aircraft suffered similar damage but the unfortunate ground crews had first to spend hours trying to get half a pound of salad cream from the interstices of the camera equipment and housing. Jerry had taken a spare sandwich in case of any hold-up.

Shortly after the Korean War started, six of our operational aircraft were allocated to the Far East. I was chosen as a member of the team to ferry them as far as San Francisco, where they were to be carrier-borne across the Pacific. Captain Rhodarmer and I led the two flights of three aircraft. There was a considerable urgency to get them there but when we landed at midday in Arizona for refuelling, Roger and I decided that it would be unwise to fly off immediately but that we should delay until the evening when the ambient temperature was much lower. The airfield was at 5,000 feet above sea level and its longest runway was only 5,000 feet off the tarmac; with the high summery temperature and the well-known poor acceleration of the RF 80, we considered a delay of about five hours would be a wise move. We signalled our revised plan to the appropriate authority but were instructed in no uncertain terms to get our rear ends into the atmosphere which the good Lord had provided. We did as ordered. Roger took his three aircraft to the runway with my second flight close behind. The first flight seemed to crawl down the flight path and No. 3 pilot called, "Abandoning take-off, speed far too low". He pulled off the runway, crashing into obstructions on the airfield, being badly injured in the process. Roger's No. 2, on his right, made a similar call and was lucky enough to travel up a fairly steep ramp being built alongside the runway. He burned out his brakes and damaged the wheels but fortunately stayed in one piece. Roger made a dicey but successful take-off and waited for the remaining aircraft to join him. I signalled my two stalwarts, who must have wondered what was going on, to adhere to their briefing instructions and then set off, hoping for more success than Roger. My No. 2 on my right kept close to me but abandoned his take-off early enough to be able to stop before the end of the runway. He caught up with us later. My No. 3 followed the example of Roger's No. 3 but didn't crash into anything, merely damaging the undercarriage in the process of slowing down. We should, of course, have disregarded the instructions of the higher authority and taken off individually, joining up once airborne, but the concise orders were so explicit that it seemed impossible to disobey. My own take-off was quite exciting too, as I approached the end of the runway I realised that I was going to hit a low wall about 50 yards beyond the tarmac so I raised the wheels and, luckily, they came up quickly and we missed the wall. This airfield had been built on top of a slight hill and I was able to lower the nose and build up speed by flying down a narrow gully. Strangely, I heard no more about this incident, nor, I believe, did Captain Rhodarmer. The US Air Force had lost three aircraft which should have gone straight to the war zone and one trained reconnaissance pilot consigned to hospital. Very likely, when the matter was aired at a board of enquiry the authorities combined apparent ignorance of the effects of high summer temperatures at midday, the lower air pressure at 5,000 feet above sea level, and an airfield with short runways. The subject should have been dropped.

After about a month at Shaw Field I received a letter from the South Carolina Police Department. They said that since the Air Force Authorities had stated that I was to remain there for at least a year longer I would need to have a driving test with the Chief of Police and would I please present myself with my car to the Police Department on a given date. By then I had learned what was called for in their version of the Highway Code and I'd had some experience of driving on the right of the road. So with no trepidation and a complete ignorance of the severe penalties involved should I fail, I presented myself at the Police Station and stated why I was there. The Chief of Police soon joined me and we set off with him sitting on my right. Presumably with the aim of letting me settle down and calm my nerves in the presence of the Big White Chief he asked me questions about my stay in the States, my experiences in the Second World War etc. On frequent occasions I asked him what he wanted me to do for the test and he always said, "Just drive on". Finally, after at least thirty minutes driving he said we'd better go back because he had other tests to do that afternoon. I said, "What about this test?" He replied, "Oh, that's O.K. – I just loved hearing you talk!"

# 18. Cigars All Round

IN JANUARY 1950 our son Christopher was born, an occurrence of sheer delight to Sheila who now had a real live doll to play with. Because we were in a military organisation, Bunty was registered in the US Army Hospital in Columbia, South Carolina, half an hour's drive from our home in Sumter. As we rolled up to the army base we had a puncture right at the gates of the guardroom and we were very impressed by the efficiency of the army personnel. In no time Bunty was whisked off at speed down the main drive to the Maternity Unit in a jeep, bouncing, uncomfortably for sure, siren blaring and the base tannoy system declaring an emergency and banning all traffic from movement on the main route to the hospital. Moreover, the Army Police took me under their wing and arranged for the motor pool to mend the puncture. I was then taken to the Officers' Mess to await news of Bunty's welfare. The car was returned to me, puncture repaired and polished inside and out! Chris is now an American citizen whenever he steps onto American soil – a condition of dual nationality which he may claim if ever he needs to or wants to. He had an obligation to undergo military service at his coming-of-age, as all American's have, but this was waived in his case when he joined the R.A.F. Reserve in the University Air Squadron at St. Andrews. When I returned to the squadron the next morning it was a case of cigars all round, for the men, a strong American custom when a boy is born – I don't know but it might be flowers or chocolates all round if it's a girl.

In November 1950 I was offered the opportunity of ferrying a brand new T-33 jet trainer from Los Angeles, to our squadron at Shaw Field.

Naturally, I jumped at the task and one of my colleagues mentioned that the fastest passage west to east for a single-engine aircraft was a few years back and that a T-33 could easily beat this record, especially since it would only require two refuelling stops.

I arrived in LA by commercial airline and checked in at the Lockheed plant. One of their test pilots had carried out a short air test on the T-33 I was required to deliver so I worked out my flight-plan to fly back east with stops to refuel at Albuquerque and Oklahoma City. I'd take off late afternoon and be back at base by the early hours of the next morning, hopefully having broken the west-to-east record for the honour of the squadron.

The flight to Albuquerque was uneventful, the last hour being flown in the dark. A quick refuelling took place and I was airborne again for Oklahoma City. For the last hundred miles or so of this leg I became aware of some very powerful-looking electrical storms ahead, stretching from as far north as I could see, to many hundreds of miles south of my track. I landed at Oke City and was able to get some first-hand information of the weather ahead of me from a B-29 pilot who had just come through it. He told me that the line squall was quite energetic but he had managed to find a gap to fly through at 35,000 feet. He considered that the frontal storms were developing and that my passage through it would be somewhat turbulent. It was about one hundred miles east of the airfield and I should be able to climb above it if I acted quickly.

I took off about midnight and climbed as rapidly as possible. The line squall was clearly active with lightning flashes throughout its length. I had reached 39,000 feet and was a few miles short of the nearest cloud which bubbled and flashed above me. I entered the top of the cloud at 42,000 feet and decided, belatedly, to turn on the pitot head heater. If I had thought about it, of course, the ice crystals forming the cloud would present no threat to the airspeed indicator system so I didn't really need the heater on – pilots are taught to turn on the heater whenever they enter cloud so that ice cannot form in the pitot head. However, I took out my torch to select the correct switch from the bank of switches on my right hand side, I located 'PIT HTR,' switched it 'ON' and the engine stopped.

112

I knew there was no hope of returning to Oklahoma City and, in any case, the bad weather was moving in that direction. The best plan was to continue on course because a line squall, although hundreds of miles in length, was usually somewhat narrow and I had already reached the centre of this one, judging by the turbulence and ferocity of the lightning flashes. I hoped to relight the engine and continue my flight back to Shaw Field. I might still manage to get there within the record time. I trimmed the aircraft for a glide descent and drew out my maps to check on the local terrain and the nearest available airfields in case the plan was upset. At this point I dropped my torch and it rolled away to an inaccessible part of the cockpit. However, there was enough light from the lightning flashes for me to determine that I was by now over the Ozark Mountain Plateau which, in places, reached up to 6-7,000 feet above sea level. My nearest available airfield was Birmingham in Alabama.

I was aware that the type of engine fitted to the T-33 would not normally relight above 25,000 feet but I made my first attempt at 28,000 hoping that, if the relight was successful, I still might break the record. It was unsuccessful. I changed the radio transmitter to the Emergency channel and made a MAYDAY call, giving all the details required but, due to the excessive cracklings and static interference on the radio because of the line squall, I heard no reply.

At 21,000 feet I made my second relight attempt but that was also fruitless. This was getting serious. I then decided to make one more attempt, this time at 15,000 feet and bale out at 10,000 feet if I had no luck because I figured (Americanese creeping in) I'd need at least 2,000 feet clearance above ground to make a safe descent. I was still in cloud but the lightning flashes were getting less frequent. My next effort to get the engine going was also unsuccessful so I made preparations to abandon the aircraft. I made a final MAYDAY call indicating my intention to jump. Again, I heard no reply due to interference. At this stage, all thought of a record-breaking flight had disappeared. Survival was paramount.

At 11,000 feet, one last, almost despairing attempt to regain power was made and, glory be, the engine responded. I gingerly increased the power and checked round the cockpit to make sure that temperatures and pressures were back to normal. At 9,000 feet, I came out of cloud leaving the storms behind and sat back to admire the, to me, heavenly sight of the odd light down below.

I cancelled my MAYDAY call and requested a course to steer me to the nearest military airfield. Control gave me a heading and said that Maxwell Field was ready to receive me. On landing at Maxwell I was led into the dispersal area by the most frightening monster of the fire-fighting vehicle I'd ever seen. It dwarfed my aircraft and half-a-dozen keen fire-fighters were aiming their hoses at me, no doubt hoping I'd burst into flames. I reported what had happened and went to bed after receiving an assurance the aircraft would be subjected to a close inspection.

The next morning I was told that the T-33 was now fully serviceable and that the cause of the engine failure was a wrongly routed electrical switch. The pitot head heater had been connected to the emergency engine relight system and vice versa. This meant that the engine had been doused with a gallon or more fuel when the burners were at their lowest flame at 42,000 ft. That would certainly put out the fire. I flew back to base at Shaw, fully expecting to be hung, drawn and quartered because the USAF had a strict rule that an aircraft on a ferry or delivery flight was not to be flown under instrument conditions and not at night. I had violated two regulations at least.

When I taxied into the squadron dispersal I was ready for the worst – they might even send me back to the UK. However, I received a tumultuous welcome with much hand-shaking and back-slapping and comments on a splendid piece of airmanship and skill for having had an engine failure at over 40,000 feet in a thunderstorm and bringing the plane in safely on a 'dead-stick' landing.

Naturally, I said nothing at the time but was later taken quietly aside by the CO who gave me a gentle rocket for disobeying standing orders. He said he was sorry not to have had the pleasure of being the CO of a record-breaking squadron but he was very glad I was back in one piece with a new aircraft and that he didn't have to break the news of a tragic accident to Bunty. He certainly knew how to strike home with even a gentle rebuke.

I knew that Americans were well committed to the never-never system of credit buying but my eyes were opened when I found the depth to which hire purchase had invaded their way of life. The Officers' Pay Parade was held monthly from a caravan built especially for this event. Steps were built on both sides of the vehicle; the officers would enter on one side, be paid in cash and would be prepared, as he came down the other side, to find his wife waiting with a list of HP debts that had to be paid. Radio, phonograph or music centre, washing machine, tumble dryer, hair dryer, butcher, baker, hot-dog maker – the list must have seemed endless. Then there would be petrol for the car, food for the month, rent, insurances, and holiday plans etc. etc. When all known debts were covered there would be cash for a hair-do, pocket money for herself and the children, and many other known monthly outgoings. What was left was his to spend. I never noticed any evidence of a desire to save; maybe that was one of the effects of the HP system. Certainly, parties flourished for a week or so after a pay parade but dried up completely until the next one. At one point, Bunty and I decided to buy a small clock radio. I went into Sumter, chose a suitable instrument and said I'd like to pay by HP. The shopkeeper asked for my name and how long I'd been in the district. I told him and he went away to the phone. When he returned he said with some reluctance that he was sorry but the local Chamber of Commerce stated that I had a 'Zero Credit Rating'. This meant, apparently, that with a zero or low credit rating I was possibly guilty of fraud or of never paying fully any HP instalments. Credit Rating was a safeguard for the shopkeeper. He beamed when I said I'd never used HP before, I'd always paid cash. I obtained the radio on the never-never but did not use it again.

Our two-year tour in the States was nearing its end and many of our evenings were taken up by kind invitations to farewell parties from the squadron members and their wives. All the Americans throughout our stay were most kind and considerate. The USAF was also keen to show its feelings by arranging to get the car back to the UK for free by either military cargo or even by strapping it to the deck of an aircraft carrier going that way.

I am sure that a large share of the affection shown was due to the presence of Sheila with her charms, and Christopher with his fair curly hair and blue, blue eyes. It was just as well that we were on board the Queen Mary and a few hundred miles away when Sheila, no doubt with real love and affection, deprived Christopher of every one of his beautiful golden curls.

115

# 19. Another Real Live Doll

OUR RETURN TO THE UK on the Queen Mary was a luxury with the staff only too keen to help with Chris and Sheila with whom they clearly fell in love. We knew we were heading, in just five days, to the austerity which still ruled the UK. The weather there was going to be very different from what we'd been experiencing during the last two years in the southern States. Nevertheless, it would be wonderful to be back with our own families again and, as for Sheila and Chris, nothing would be too good for them. We were due two weeks leave prior to my next posting and we were keen to get up-to-date with news of our relatives and friends.

At my interview in London I was told that as I had been flying since joining the Air Force I would be on a 'ground tour' for at least the next two years. I had been expecting this to happen – I just hoped I'd get a posting to a unit which had an airfield and some aircraft available. I was lucky – I was consigned to R.A.F. Benson (of all places) which was housing the formation of a new OCU, No. 231, which was destined to occupy R.A.F. Bassingbourn near Royston in Hertfordshire. This station had been occupied by the US Air Force as a transport and staging post for their Army and Air Force commitments.

No. 231 OCU was planned to be the new training base for crews who would be operational in Canberra aircraft, the famed new light/medium bomber jet for the R.A.F. I was scheduled to be the Chief Ground Instructor of the Unit's Ground School. Our duties would start as soon as the Americans had departed.

117

Whilst at Benson I managed to persuade the OC Flying to let me take the station Tiger Moth to Scotland to visit Bunty and the children who had gone north to wait until I could find accommodation near Bassingbourn. This was an epic flight for me because the Tiger's speed in forward motion was 95 mph in still air and on my return journey I had a 50 knot headwind to contend with. While dashing like a bullet through Northumberland I noticed a southbound express below – a minute later he was well ahead of me. What a disgrace! In October of that year my new unit moved to R.A.F. Bassingbourn and I settled down as CGI to build up the Ground School. Fortunately I had a wonderful Flight Sergeant on my staff who had done this sort of thing before. Chiefy Sparks could turn his hand to any task; he had a method of obtaining equipment almost immediately which was unobtainable anywhere else without a lengthy period of waiting. He also had eight young children and needed two married quarters to house them.

About this time I was promoted to the dizzy height of the rank of Squadron Leader but that didn't help in the married quarters stakes because there were no MQs available at that time for senior officers. So we were back on the house-hunting lark. Good fortune was with us again, especially since our third child was soon due. We were able to get very good accommodation in a large vicarage in Litlington, a small village a few miles from the airfield. The vicar was responsible for the religious guidance of two other village communities beside Litlington and I have often wondered how he was able to because of his background. He was an erudite theologian from a senior religious college and very likely had no real background or foundation for looking after the religious or social requirements of a rural parish, let alone three. He was a charming person and was thoroughly delighted at the prospect of having two young children in his vicarage and, in due course, a baby to join them. In addition to his parochial duties he was padre to the R.A.F. station at Duxford and took great delight and pride in taking Sheila with him on his regular visits. She knew her reading books by heart from start to end and would sit beside him in the car and read him fairy tales as if she'd just picked up the book for the first time.

At this stage Christopher was just over two years old and when he was told a new baby was soon to join us his immediate reaction was to say,

"Oh no, not another one. I just hope it's a boy". When Maralyn arrived he looked closely at her, poked her and said with a sigh, "Oh no, take her back and get a boy". Sheila, on the other hand, was thrilled and delighted because she now had another real live doll to look after.

I was returning from work one day and as I passed the open door of the church I saw Sheila on her tricycle speeding up and down the aisle. I called her out at once and said, "You must not ride inside the church, you've got plenty of room outside". A voice from within said, "Of course she can ride inside the church. God's house is open for all who wish to enter, whatever the reason and whatever the time". Another time some workers were painting the outer walls of the building and one of them was high up on a ladder. Two-and-a-half year-old Christopher called out, "What you doing, Charlie?" And sure enough, one of them (I guessed it must have been Charlie) came all the way down and spent minutes explaining to him just what each worker was up to.

By May 1953 I had managed to find the time to convert on to the Canberra aircraft – to my mind a 'gentleman's jet' compared with other jets I had flown. Bassingbourn was provided at first with the basic B2 bomber version, not by any means the ideal type for a training unit. The cockpit was big enough for the pilot and navigator with space to reach the entry/exit hatch. There was a wooden flap seat for the instructor just above the hatch and I, for one, was not very happy at the possibility of having to abandon the aircraft quickly in an emergency with the navigator right behind me and the student pilot struggling for control. Particularly at night. We all waited eagerly for the T4 trainer to come on line with its dual controls and ejection seats. The Canberra was obviously the up-and-coming aircraft at that time and the two training squadrons were, in August 1953, judged to be insufficient for the task of providing all the crew needed for the operational squadrons of Bomber Command. A third squadron was therefore established and to my great delight was offered to me. What joy! My ground tour was over. Bunty, Sheila, Chris and our new arrival Maralyn took over a well-equipped MQ alongside the sports field, a happy situation for all of us. At this stage, although Christopher was too young for the local council school, he desperately wanted to go to school where, he'd heard, fun and games were the norm. We managed to get them accepted at a local Convent school where

Sheila soon developed an intense love of the peaceful attitude of the staff and children. Learning the stories of Christ and the songs and hymns were just what she was interested in. Her progress reports were very good – she loved every minute. After the first week or so Christopher decided Convent life was not for him, nor was rice pudding every day an attraction, and it became increasingly difficult to get him to board the bus each morning. He still hates rice pudding!

The training staff at Bassingbourn included the Station Navigation Officer, a very experienced and likeable Flight Lieutenant whose surname was Nightingale. Naturally, as in all similar situations, he was given the friendly soubriquet of 'Flossie'. He did not seem to mind but privately he must have been very tired of it. When he returned from leave on one occasion he took the opportunity, one Saturday lunchtime in the Officer's Mess bar (the right and proper location to make for at the end of a busy working week), to make an announcement. He said he had taken the opportunity to visit Somerset House during his leave and had officially changed his surname to Newton and he requested that this move on his part would be respected in the future. Our immediate reaction in the bar was to say, "Newton, yes, we like it. Goes well with Flossie. Flossie Newton. Sounds good".

One of the instructors in my squadron, Laurie Harrington, was a most resourceful individual. He realised that the very fast-burning, almost explosive material which made up the Canberra engine starter cartridges could be sawn into slices (like pineapple slices). He got boot polish tins and other containers of similar proportions, put a nut and bolt through the centre and bored two holes off-set on opposite sides of the bottom of the tin and fitted two short pieces of fuse in the holes. This, he reckoned, should make a suitable firework for November 5th or for that matter, any day of the year. The maiden flight of this heavier-than-air machine was completely successful. With both fuses lit it began to rotate within two seconds and shot up 300 feet with a most satisfactory banshee howl. We made many of these devices and had no failures at all. It soon became well known and was universally approved, except by the Senior Air Traffic Control Officer (SATCO) whose perimeter taxi tracks had been resurfaced with tarmac. We were so sure of the performance of our vehicle that we invited all the station personnel to a demonstration on the first Saturday morning when the flying programme finished. We prepared a dozen or more for the shoe and paraded them out on the airfield. The Station Commander, the Padre and most of the flying types arrived together with dozens of other interested onlookers and formed a wide circle around the 'operating area' of the perimeter track. We let off a few of the show polish tins as a starter followed by some larger ones made from furniture polish tins etc. which made much more noise, flew much higher and evoked suitable 'oohs' and 'ahhs' from the assembled throng. One of the smaller of the exhibits, from a shoe polish tin, was fitted with a twist-grip device on its side (for easier opening). This was unfortunate – or not, depending on your view of the sanctity of members of Religious Orders – because this one proved to be the most popular among the members of the audience. It began normally, like the others, developed its maximum rotation in half a second and leapt into the air. It appears that the twist-grip device on the circumference of the tin couldn't stand the immense strain and it failed, allowing the internal gases to discover a third exit. This caused the tin to change its direction at about two feet above the ground. It turned to the horizontal and sped with increasing velocity and its banshee wail towards the Station Padre. Fortunately, for him at least, he was watching it closely. He realised at once the importance of developing rapid upward reactions and he leapt upward, with legs wide apart, at a speed rarely seen in 'a man of the cloth'. I was unable to tell whether the ensuing vociferous applause was for man or machine.

Finally, we presented two actual heavy starter cartridges to which we had fitted metal propellers or blades – rather like a helicopter in appearance. The first began quite slowly on its rotational career. After a few seconds it took off and rose majestically to the greatest height yet achieved. The second, unfortunately, had been fitted with its propeller reversed. This meant that as soon as the speed of rotation increased it tended to move downwards. The bottom of this exhibit was of course hot and getting hotter by the second. This final performance intrigued all the spectators except the SATCO who was seen to be dancing up and down with rage and frustration as he saw his beautiful newly-tarmac-covered peritrack being eaten by an unstoppable monster. The new surface hadn't yet hardened and our downward helicopter dug deep. Altogether we felt that our first public venture had been a success – only two per cent (approx.) did not achieve full satisfaction from the occasion.

# 20. WHO, THEN, DID THEY BURY?

THE BOMBING RANGE used by the Bassingbourn crews was a field near Thetford normally occupied by a herd of cattle. When practice bombing was scheduled the farmer would be informed by the Flying Staff and he would clear the animals out. After all, nobody would like to endanger these defenceless creatures. It would be abominable.

One of the more serious problems which faced Canberra crews was the occasional malfunction of the electrical trimming device fitted at the top of the control column. It was a four-positioned switch, left or right to adjust to trimming on the wings, forward and back to do the same on the elevator. The aim of the trimmer is to reduce the aerodynamic load on the control column and thus to reduce pilot fatigue. The early Canberras were occasionally subject to run-away trimmers and unless the pilot was able to react quickly, the full extent of the trimmer would be imposed in seconds.

One trainee crew on a practice bombing mission were killed when their aircraft nose-dived into the ground from a medium height close to the target. Two of the three crewmen were found in the wreckage but the third was missing. It was clearly a case of a run-away forward trimmer. We attended three funerals that week. I then learned how desperately unpleasant and despicable the average journalist or editor can be, completely ignoring the grief and misery of the relatives and others just to sell a 'copy'. Apparently, the farmer who owned the field where the accident took place stopped for his lunch and decided to sit above a ditch at the edge of the field. He noticed a bright yellow object at the bottom of the ditch which he then investigated.

It was of course the flying jacket of the third crew member and the unfortunate crewman was also there. The authorities were informed and, naturally, the farmer's story was the principal topic in his local pub that lunchtime. The subject matter was passed to a local tabloid journalist and the next morning his newspaper produced a 'screaming' headline in large print – WHO, THEN, DID THEY BURY?

One day I was asked to carry out a height climb on a Canberra T4 trainer to at least 45,000 ft. We did manage to get to 51,000 ft. (just under ten miles high) but by then the aircraft was struggling, nose high above the horizon, getting close to a stall. The rate of climb was less than 200 ft. per minute and it seemed pointless to try to get any higher. It was a perfect day and the visibility allowed us to see parts of the west coast of England and a glimpse of Ireland from our position over London.

My future in Bomber Command seemed very promising – a jet instructor, the rank of Squadron Leader with experience of the Command's excellent new light bomber-to-be at a time when the V-force of heavy bombers (Vulcan, Valiant and Victor) was developing. However, this was not to be. It was October 1954.

A hundred miles or so to the north, two Squadron Leaders, each in charge of a Meteor training squadron in Flying Training Command, had a stand-up fight in the bar one evening. This took place in front of a group of officers including student pilots. The Group Captain Station Commander, quite rightly, ordered them off his station within twenty-four hours. The Air Ministry Personnel staff had to search immediately for two replacements. They found one (whose family soon became very good friends with ours) within the Command but the only available 'creature' in the Air Force to fit the posting was, apparently, a certain officer in command of 'C' Squadron at Bassingbourn. Once more the Durbidge family were moving, this time to wildest Nottinghamshire and into the welcoming arms of Flying Training Command.

# 21. A Happy Posting

R.A.F. WORKSOP was my target that weekend so I polished the car, cleaned and fiddled about with the engine in order to arrive in style. In the process of fiddling, I cleaned the ignition system and on returning the rotor arm to its rightful position I did not take sufficient care. The rotor arm shattered into four or five pieces as soon as I tried to start the engine. Panic took over. No remedy, so I got hold of our Squadron Magician, Laurie Harrington, and presented him with the broken bits. I was due to take off for Worksop the next morning and certainly expected to advise them that I'd be delayed somewhat. After all, what chance was there of getting a replacement rotor arm for an American V-8 engine late on a Saturday evening? I was so lucky to have Laurie Harrington on my side because early next morning he appeared with the rotor arm rebuilt. A true magician. He had used gardening twine and carpenters glue and had baked it all night. The arm fitted perfectly and the engine started on the first go. Laurie said there was a garage on my route which specialised in spares for American motors and if I got that far I could get a replacement. I did get that far; I did get a spare arm and determined I would change them over when the Harrington Arm failed. It never did. The spare arm was still in the glove compartment when the car was handed over many years later.

R.A.F. Worksop, home of No. 211 Flying Training School, turned out to be a wartime airfield with very good facilities for flying but little for peacetime habitation. No married quarters, just one house which was occupied by the Wing Commander in charge of flying, one Ronnie Knott, about the most pleasant, enthusiastic 'boss' an instructor could wish for. The Station Commander, another 'gem', lived off the station. All the buildings were Nissen Huts but the whole place worked efficiently and happily. It seemed strange to have half a Nissen Hut to sleep in once again with my own coke stove for warmth. The Officers' Mess looked like a labyrinthine London Underground Station and, in fact, was decorated as such for the Summer Ball. For me, it was a happy posting.

I started my usual immediate search for somewhere for the five of us to live and this is where my 'stock' reached its nadir. I found a pleasant house late one evening not far from the airfield and located just opposite the fine wrought-iron gates of a hospital. An infant school nearby (Sheila was five by now) and in a quiet neighbourhood. We moved in; the next morning, we answered a knock on the door and a uniformed man said, "Don't take your children to school today. Keep your doors shut. Not to be answered to anyone. Don't let the children play outside and keep a poker or something by the door. The 'hammer murderer' has escaped. We'll let you know when it is safe again". We had taken up residence just at the gates of the Rampton Criminal Lunatic Asylum. We did stay there a short time, long enough to entertain Bunty's mother and sister and to make preparations for Christmas – the inmates were good postal workers, salesmen and parcel handlers – but fortunately we were provided with a MQ at R.A.F. Finningley which had been closed for runway resurfacing and conversion to a V-Force station.

Worksop was a very busy unit and all four Meteor squadrons were fully occupied especially when we would receive unscheduled batches of eight or ten semi-trained National Service airmen who had been promised full training to Wings standard. The Air Ministry was at that time experimenting with the idea of civilianising aspects of Air Force life, obviously to economise – an airman must be paid, fed, clothed, housed, kept fit and healthy etc., a civilian employee doing the same job just needs to be paid.

Worksop was chosen to have its stores section civilianised soon after I took over No. 4 Squadron. As CO I was of course responsible for the complete inventory of equipment including eight Meteors and all the hangar equipment etc., valued, I suppose, at some millions of pounds and the now civilianised department quite sensibly asked me to do an inventory check.

When it was completed I was charged a total of sixpence – I was short of a blackboard duster. One of the new Equippers said I should have substituted a rag from the hangar floor – clearly a clever lad; he'll go far.

Squadron Leader Sam Wilding was the R.A.F. Commander of this Equipment Section and he and his wife Pearl became our firm friends. Later, the first line servicing of the aircraft and the day-to-day handling of all ground aspects of the flying were civilianised and handed over to Airwork Services Ltd. – again a very successful move. By then we were flying Vampires for final Wings training and the Vampire T4 was the instructional machine, with side-by-side seating and ejection seats. Several very strict rules are in force when jump seats are fitted – safety first with explosives. I scheduled myself to fly with a student on the first detail so that I could determine for myself the adequacy of the Airwork takeover.

A fresh-faced young man leapt up onto the wing of the Vampire, helped me to adjust the safety strap, withdrew the safety pin from the ejection seat, showed it to me in the correct manner and then placed it in the special pocket. I was glad to see he had completed the task in the approved order and I said to him, "Thank you, that's fine – do you think you are going to enjoy this new job, and how long have you been working with aeroplanes?" He said, "Oh yes, I like it very well. The pay is better too. We were given instruction during the whole weekend. This is much better than the Army". I then asked him when he'd left the Army and which had been his regiment. He said, "I left last week. I was in The Pioneer Corps". When we returned from that flight a different man jumped up on the wing, withdrew the safety pin from its pocket, showed it to me and, placing it in its slot in the seat firing tube said, "Safety pin in and secure, Sir". I thanked him and asked if he was on engines. He said, "Oh, I've been on engines all my life. I love them diesels".

For obvious safety reasons transferring control of an aircraft from one pilot to another must be done with clear precision. Officially, the words "You have control" answered by "I have control" should be used. After many, many years of using this formula I began to slip into the habit of saying, "You've got it" or "I've got it" instead. I learned my lesson at Worksop. I combined an air test with a student exercise and when both were done I suggested he should do me some aerobatics on the way back to base, starting with a slow roll.

We were at about 5,060 feet, he did one roll and in the inverted position a large, heavy pair of pliers landed on the cockpit canopy from the cockpit floor. I could not catch it in time. I told the student to do another slow roll and this time I caught the pliers. I said, "I've got it", meaning the pair of pliers. The student released control of the aircraft thinking I'd meant to take over. From this inverted position the Meteor soon built up a dangerous high speed dive. When the aircraft began to shudder I asked the student what he was playing at. He said, "You said you'd got it, Sir, so I released control".

Towards the end of a Wings course the poor student is subjected to many tests both on the ground and in the air. One of these tests is the Night Navigation Flight. My student was doing quite well, his technique, knowledge etc., was up to the required standard and we were en route to base from Newcastle. All was quiet. It was well after midnight and I had heard hardly a sound during the last fifteen minutes except perhaps the gentle swish of the air over the canopy and the soft murmur of the two Derwent engines. In fact, it was so quiet that I thought perhaps the radio receiver was not working properly. I knew the intercom was O.K. but became suspicious of the radio transmitter/receiver. The best way to check was to press the transmit button for a second and listen for the 'click'. I did this, got my 'click' and a voice said, "OO DAT?" A pause and I said, "OO DAT SAY OO DAT?" The voice said, "OO DAT UP DER?" I said, "OO DAT DOWN DER SAY OO DAT UP HERE?" This went on for a few minutes with variations from other Worksop aircraft on the same frequency. Eventually the Officer in command at Worksop told us to cut it out, and for heaven's sake come home so he could get to bed.

I recall another amusing incident when the 'training on instruments' part of the course was reached. Worksop only had CRDF as a let-down aid for practice and for bad weather approaches to the runway. However, we did have an arrangement with an American base at Sturgate, near Gainsborough in Lincolnshire, about 25miles away, for us to practise bad weather approaches and landings using their Ground Controlled Approach equipment (CGA). Their operators were most efficient and when they were not busy with their own aircraft movements they would search for business from training units like us.

I remember getting airborne from base with a student who was due to carry out practice instrument approach procedures and whom I had briefed on CGA type approaches. We changed R/T channels just after take-off and a voice said, "If the aircraft just airborne from Worksop wishes to carry out CGA approaches at Sturgate, steer 080 degrees and climb 2,000 ft". I replied, "Sturgate, this is Kilo Delta, turning onto 080 degrees, will call you on course at 2,000 ft".

There followed a very useful exercise during which I demonstrated two CGA approaches, one visual and one on instruments, both obeying implicitly the instructions of the Controller on the ground. Then I explained to my student that he would fly the next one visually checking instrument indications and noting how the controller nursed the aircraft round the circuit. We did quite well and on the next run I told him to fly it on instruments but I would do all the radio calls, leaving him to concentrate on the accuracy of his flying. On the downwind leg the Controller said, "Kilo Delta, you are advised that on this next approach your descent will be under the control of a trainee controller. If you are not satisfied at any time with the instructions given you are to take overshoot action and climb away". I said, "Sturgate, you are advised that this next approach will be flown by a trainee pilot, please take whatever action you deem necessary if you are in any way unhappy with the approach pattern". The reply was, "Ahm getting outta here".

The Training staff at Worksop tried hard to complete the weekly flying programme in five days, Monday to Friday, leaving Saturday mornings free for odd jobs like air tests, student reports, logbook checks and general briefings and preparations for the next week's work. One day, no doubt in the bar, the idea was put forward to use one Saturday morning to launch an all-instructor Balbo i.e. a large formation of aircraft – named after an early Italian military aircraft enthusiast who was the first to organise and lead such a gathering, perhaps, going, as they say, same way, same day.

This suggestion was received with enthusiasm by all the instructors – getting aloft without a student to look after was an excellent notion. Ronnie Knott, the Chief Instructor, approved the idea on condition that: a) each of the four squadrons would provide four Meteors plus one spare; b) the Balbo would be led and controlled by the youngest instructor on the station and he, the Chief Instructor would fly at No. 16, tail-end Charlie, the last to take-off and to land; c) each Squadron Commander would fly at No. 4 in his own section of four aircraft which would be led by the squadron's newest instructor; d) the Balbo leader was to plan and execute a 50-minute flight obeying all flight rules and instructions from Air Traffic Control, avoiding all danger areas and high ground and not flying below 500 feet. He would also be responsible for the pre-flight briefing and after-flight summary. What a chance to make his name on the station!

The whole operation went according to plan. The young leader chose a route for the Balbo which, among other targets, took us directly over R.A.F. Swinderby, a sister jet-training station, at a height of 500 ft. NOISY, with thirty-two jet engines overhead all at once. No doubt he'd thought to fly the Worksop flag or perhaps to boast that we could get sixteen Meteors serviceable at any one time. Our passage over Swinderby took place at 11:00am.

All the members of the Balbo thoroughly enjoyed the exercise, not least Ronnie Knott, I should imagine the happiest was the young man who had done an excellent job and had got us all back in safely and all together.

There were sequels to this – we were unable to repeat this experiment at Worksop due to the pressure of work and the influx of a score of unscheduled extra students. However, we learned some weeks later that Swinderby had taken up the challenge and had determined to repay the compliment but at an earlier time overhead. Unfortunately for them, they had assumed that the Balbo had come from Cranwell. A contest developed between them with the fly-past times getting earlier and earlier. We wondered how early the contestants and their unfortunate ground crews would have had to get up to be overhead by, say, 0800 hrs. It was very satisfactory to lie back in bed and dream.

The instructors at Worksop tried to put on a light amusement for staff and students just prior to Christmas. Cinderossella, a fun-filled tribute to Tony Ross, one of the best of them, was to have been enacted on two nights but very dense fog prevented all but the living-in folk from attending. Driving back to our Married Quarter at R.A.F. Finningley, Bunty and I were followed by a car which stuck so closely to my tail I knew the driver would not let me go. That particular part of the A1, as it was then, was well known to me – I drove it daily and knew there was a conspicuous lay-by directly before the

R.A.F. Finningley turn-off appeared. I stopped in the lay-by, so did the car behind. I got out and went back. It was a taxi, full of giggling, hysterical girls all vowing never to go to a party again. The poor taxi driver looked a trifle distraught but I explained that I was about to turn off right into Finningley and not to follow me further. I could no longer help them. The driver said, "Well, thanks for this far. I know the rest of the road to Doncaster". I certainly didn't envy him. I just hope he got paid.

# 22. Nowt But Shops

MY FIRST 'DESK JOB' had been short and had ended with a fine flying job on Canberras. Not so lucky this time – nor for the rest of my R.A.F. career. After the good two years at Worksop, and I really mean good, we were posted to No.23 Group Headquarters at R.A.F. Stanbridge, near Leighton Buzzard in Bedfordshire. No.23 Group supervised both Piston and Jet engined flying training in the UK. My share was the four jet stations, thankfully I did know a bit about them. There were flying visits to be done and we were allocated an Anson, a Meteor, a Vampire and a Provost, (standard piston-engined trainer) all based a few miles away at Cranfield. I should perhaps explain that all flying personnel within the Air Force are required, or were then, to maintain a minimum standard of their airborne capabilities, even on a 'ground' tour. If I recall correctly, the flying time required was 2 hours per month – not much from my point of view. I did manage to get 170 hours in at 23 Group during my 2 year stay, mainly by volunteering for any visits by non-aircrew personnel. Anything to get me away from the desk.

R.A.F. Stanbridge was small, more of a 'married quarter' unit than a station but it did house a Signals Unit. We were happily set up on a square portion of the camp with very good neighbours. Chris's main plan in his spare time was to race round the square on his cycle with me timing him. He'd disappear at high speed and pass me even faster for the timing run. If I gave him the thumbs up his legs would change gear into piston-locomotive mode. On one circuit he didn't appear so I went round to investigate. He'd gone round the far corner, head down, slap bang into an on-coming car and came to rest on the bonnet staring with surprise through the windscreen at an equally surprised driver. He broke his arm on this one. The hospital strapped and plastered him with strict instructions to rest. He obeyed for two days but couldn't stand it for longer, especially when he found what a good cricket bat his plaster made.

Like many olde worlde small English towns, Leighton Buzzard had a short, wide central high street with nowt but shops. Wherever you stood there was a pungent, glorious smell of smoking or grinding coffee beans. Nothing like it! It was at Stanbridge that we acquired a goldfish. We got him from some distance away and en route home he leapt out of his temporary shallow dish onto the car floor. Luckily, we had just crossed a stream where adjustments were made with the assistance of two passing motorists who'd heard the children's screaming. Goldie, their name, lived a long and precarious existence. His home was a large glass bowl or globe which lived on a wide windowsill in the MQ lounge. One winter it was so cold overnight that he was found the next morning lying on his side in an inch of water with six inches of ice above him. The next summer, same place, he got so hot that his golden scales turned to silver; but he was no silverfish. We won a much smaller goldfish at a fair much later; our over-joyed children settled down to choose a new name for Goldie's companion. They wasted their time. We put him in with Goldie to keep him company but Goldie ate him that first night. At least, there was no sign of him in the morning, the water was very discoloured and Goldie looked fatter. CANNIBAL! He survived many years and we finally gave him away on our new posting to Germany in June 1959.

Moving from one R.A.F. station to another was no problem at all for me. All I had to do was to dump my gear into the big Ford and go. It was poor Bunty I was sorry for. The final clear-up, the handing over of the MQ to the housing officer, checking the inventory and getting all the clothes, toys etc. of three children and herself organised, then shepherding everything to pastures new. She always managed it and apparently with ease. The Ford was perfection. Switch on and zoom away. So different from cars we had in the past. In 1947 we had an old upright Standard, like a honky-tonk piano, square and forbidding but beautifully upholstered in leather and with a very deep-stroke engine. I always parked it overnight on a gradient somewhere because it had no starter – wartime effect – and I'd lost the winding handle in the snow. Bunty and I went shopping in Newcastle and parked in the main street at Boots. In those days the law forbade leaving a car unattended with the engine running, so I waited while Bunty went into Boots to change a book (Boots's bigger shops had a lending library then). We changed over and Bunty guarded the car while I chose a book but she suddenly remembered the need for a new toothbrush. Fatal. When I went out there was the policeman with his book already writing. He gave me the ticket and disappeared. A week later, same place, my favourite bobby stopped me (I was in uniform) and said, "I'm very sorry I gave you a ticket last week, I didn't know you were R.A.F., I was too, but I had already started writing and daren't stop. I forgot to get your full name and address – could you please tell me now?" I did so, though I was later told I need not have said a thing. My first, and I stress, only appearance in court, followed some weeks later at Newcastle Magistrates' Court. The rest was sheer farce.

I stood in the dock in full R.A.F. uniform and the Magistrate asked the Clerk of Court to read the charge. "You are charged that, on the 3rd day of May 1947, at the city and county of Newcastle-upon-Tyne, being the person in charge of a certain motor vehicle, unlawfully did quit the vehicle on Northumberland Street, without having stopped the engine and having set the brake so as to effectually prevent at least two of the wheels from revolving, contrary to the Regulation make on that behalf, and to the statute in such case made and provided. How do you plead?" I said, "Not guilty". Three errors in the charge sheet were made so I pled not guilty to each, explaining why on each. The Magistrate asked me if I objected to the charge sheet being altered the three times and I said no. Finally the corrected charge was read and I pleaded guilty! "Fined two pounds," said the big boss, "please pay at the back of the Court."

A police Sergeant at the pay desk said, "I enjoyed all that. Not often we get much fun here. I'll bet someone in the Orderly Room will suffer tomorrow".

This was built to provide Headquarters facilities for British, French, Dutch, Belgian and German Air Force personnel, as well as representatives from naval, army and civilian organisations. The R.A.F. Mess was huge and it had a bar to match, about 25 yards long. I arrived late one evening, clung to the bar and ordered a whiskey with ginger ale – my favourite pick-me-up at that time – I've since got rid of the ginger. I was served by an ex-U-boat Commander who asked for my name. As soon as I told him he gave me my room number and handed me a letter. "Don't unpack. Drive to Eindhoven in Holland where Exercise Royal Flush is in full swing." This was the annual Tactical Reconnaissance Competition between two teams drawn from all the air forces in north-west Europe. Our combined team won Royal Flush that year but lost it the following year at Bremgarten in south-west Germany.

I remember taking a staff car to Bremgarten with our Chief Photographic Officer, Bill Cormack, a great friend of ours. Bill had two real joys in life apart from his delightful family. He liked to gamble (on a small scale, of course, considering our salaries) and thoroughly enjoyed picnicking when on a long car journey. He also enjoyed the odd gin and tonic. For his picnics he carried a hamper very cleverly fitted out with all necessities – stove; real plates and cups; fresh water in discarded gin bottles and, of course, gin and tonics. I think I was as close as I've ever been to seeing a strong, middle-aged gentleman weep when he found on one of our many picnic stops that he'd used a bottle full of gin to make the tea. The gin, of course, evaporated very rapidly on the stove and filled the air with a most unusual odour, not often experienced even at a picnic.

Overnight we stopped about half way to Bremgarten at the French Officers' Club at Baden-Baden, the world-renowned gambling casino town. It was too strong a temptation for Bill to resist and we spent the evening at the casino. As Officer-in-Charge of the R.A.F. part of Royal Flush I was carrying about 13,000 German Marks for accommodation charges, pay etc. for all our airmen on the exercises. The cash, in notes, was in a very strong steel and leather satchel strapped securely to my wrist. "Not to leave my person" until all had been paid off. Naturally, we couldn't leave Baden-Baden without sampling the casino atmosphere so we gambled a few of our own coins on the roulette wheel – lost them of course. Bill looked me hard in the eye and said, "Keith, 13,000 right now on number 26. Go on. Do it! Do it now, before you lose your nerve. 26 is my favourite number. IT WILL WIN". I said, "Bill, I've already lost my nerve and I certainly do not wish to be drummed out of the Service with dishonour or whatever". I had enough time to disgorge the Marks before the next play was called. But I didn't do it! Number 26 came up on the next throw. 350,000 Marks sitting there and I muffed it.

My task in this new posting to R.A.F. Germany Headquarters took me back to my wartime activities – photographic reconnaissance. I was designated Squadron Leader Ops Recce and had three Canberra squadrons at Brüggen, Laarbruch and Wildenrath and two single-engined jet fighter recce squadrons at Gütersloh and Jever in my charge. There was plenty of work to do. However, our family did get some excellent breaks and we travelled with ease to places on the Continent which would have been difficult to get to from the UK. We drove to Rosas on our first trip. This was a small fishing village on the Spanish Mediterranean coast about five miles from the French border. Chris adored this brief holiday and spent every available minute at the tiny harbour watching the fishermen at their chores. Most boats were fitted with lanterns which hung out above the water, attracting the fish after dark and made a most unusual and attractive sight – a flotilla of bobbing lights out to sea. We made two visits to Paris and Versailles, one most memorable journey to Rome and one to Venice staying in a hotel on the beach at Jesolo. The night before we went to Venice there was the most furious thunderstorm, a lucky break for us, because we came away with the impression of a beautifully clean and odourless water city of famous palaces and churches. At many weekends the faithful Ford took on shorter trips into Holland, the Hartz mountain region, the Rheine and Moselle rivers and, of course, the well-known motor racing circuits in Belgium and Germany. I consider that the family was very, very fortunate to have had a controlled but wandering life in its early stages and I'm sure this has contributed strongly to the high level of intelligence shown by Sheila, Christopher and Nonny. We were also very lucky to find good schools wherever we went. We had a comfortable married quarter at the Rheindahlen with free heating, taken from the sensible built-in heated under-footpath system common to many German towns. Bunty and I went to many operas during our stay – most German towns of any size had an operatic nucleus of high standard, supported when performing by professional celebrities.

## Memoirs of a High Flyer

Finally, from R.A.F. Germany, I must, with tears of woe still falling every time I think of it, record the sad demise of our beloved American Ford.... At that time, British people domiciled or working on the Continent were entitled to buy a foreign-made car and import it to the UK without tax, import dues etc. and the new Ford Cortina was a very attractive proposition being available with right-hand drive for UK use (the American Ford was left-hand drive of course, and this sometimes had great disadvantages when driving on the left). About this time I learned that my brother's car was ready for the scrapheap and he couldn't afford a replacement so I offered to lend him our big beauty and we bought a Cortina locally. Everything suddenly fell into place. I was required to attend a short one-week course in England and a colleague in the headquarters wanted his car brought out to him. Simple. I get the Ford to Eric, do a friend a favour and all travelling expenses are paid because I'm attending an official R.A.F. course.

I suppose things began to fall apart at Dover on the first stage of the plan. I was in R.A.F. uniform and drove off the ferry to the custom shed where I was dealt with by the most obnoxious individual I'd ever met (a bitter airman, perhaps, keen to get his own back once he was demobbed?). He asked to see my 'papers' concerning the car, proof of ownership, how come I'd bought it in the US, receipt for payment, papers relating to the export from USA to the UK then to Germany and now back again. I had no papers at all. Seventy minutes were spent with this man and no progress. Eventually he said he was going off duty and my case would be continued by one of his colleagues. I was constrained to ask him if he would be on duty in a week's time because I'd be driving back through Dover in a different car, that it wouldn't belong to me anyway and very likely there wouldn't be any papers. His colleague passed me through immediately. A few weeks later Eric had an argument with a bus on a country lane and lost. Apparently, the only serviceable item left of our lovely Ford was its clock. Regrettably, Eric had not taken out comprehensive insurance and all was lost – except the clock of course. Our return from R.A.F. Germany involved another Dover passage, once more in a different car, but my friendly Customs Officer was not on duty and our cardboard carton of thirteen varied spirits and liqueurs, each with a small amount removed, passed without much comment.

Our final posting in my Air Force career was to the Establishments Division of the Air Ministry in Holborn, London. A married quarter was provided in West Ruislip and fortunately for me was located near a London Underground terminus. This made my daily travelling time just less than an hour. Good schooling close by and, naturally, for Christopher's benefit, an R.A.F. hospital at Uxbridge to look after his broken bones when he fell out of a tree. 'Establishments' proved to be a complete surprise to me. I soon realised that the financial control by the Treasury over the Services was a Governmental feature first and foremost but behind the political façade was a system of control known to few. The operational side of Establishments consisted of two-man teams, a senior R.A.F. Officer and a Treasury 'nark' whose duty was to visit an R.A.F. Unit with a clear directive to cut 'running costs' by, say, 10% during the next twelve months. All Units throughout the world were visited by these teams. My particular 'parish' covered Stations in R.A.F. Germany and the Mediterranean so I considered myself very lucky – more flying at least, although as a passenger. My Treasury colleague was Freddie Whale who had been doing this type of job for years, thank heavens. He was a most remarkable person. A great sense of humour, a bottomless fund of jokes, all new to me, told with perfect control of brogue and vernacular, yet all the time subject to some internal trouble which required him to drink a pint of bull's blood, raw, twice per day. He never complained. He and I would report first to a Unit's Commander to say why we were visiting his station – he knew already, of course, bad news will always 'out', then a tour of all the various 'sections' on the Station to discuss the problem with the various section commanders. We naturally made suggestions where appropriate (Freddie's forte) and finally reported back to the Station Commander with our findings. I did not like my last tour in the Air Force, but Freddie Whale made it bearable.

On one of my Mediterranean trips I managed to smuggle a chameleon back home. We christened him Smokey, his approximate colour when he wasn't in the process of 'change'! We had a paddock of sorts at the rear of our quarter where Smokey spent much of his time and one fine day we saw him stalking a common garden daisy. After swaying from side to side as normal to get his distance measurement correct, he struck. The poor daisy did not survive but Smokey spent the next five minutes trying to spit the petals out. He stayed with us all summer and we took him into the house in winter but, with all the house flies hibernating he began to lose weight. We tried to contact someone who could give us guidance on feeding chameleons in winter, we even contacted the staff at London zoo, but no-one seemed to know. Poor Smokey survived until November but died one night in the lounge. We learned later that such creatures could be kept alive by spraying them occasionally with water throughout the winter! So simple.

One lunch time in the local pub where a colleague and I usually went, the door opened and in came Tony Hancock, the comedian and actor. He sat down at a table in the far corner, silent, even depressed perhaps. How I wished later that I'd at least bought him a pint – he'd provided me with so much amusement in the past on radio and TV. It is so difficult to know what is going on in people's minds.

I left the Air Force in June 1964 after 23 years. A few beers with friends and that was another of life's chapters closed.

# 23. Sheriff, Not Shotgun

WE MOVED NORTH for the next six years, living in Cockermouth, Cumbria. Here the children all made excellent progress in school and on the sports field. Bunty put on her teaching robes again and I had a taste of salesmanship. Selling Mr. Softy ice-cream in North-West England until the whole busipublisness was absorbed one weekend by J. Lyons Ltd. I spent two weeks on the dole – a most dispiriting sensation, and then obtained a post as an Assistant Personnel Officer with special responsibility for apprentices in a large aluminium extrusion plant called High Duty Alloys. Six very interesting years went by during which I was able to get back into flying. Many weekends I was driving over to Newcastle to fly Tiger Moths and Chipmunks with the local Air Training Corps and Newcastle University Air Squadron.

The gods took pity on me in 1970. I read an advertisement in a flying magazine calling for qualified flying instructors to serve in Singapore. What a chance! I applied immediately of course and attended the interview in Bournemouth. Who should be the interviewing Officer for Airwork Services Ltd., but Laurie Harrington, the magic manipulator of garden twine and carpenter's glue from Canberra days, sitting behind an enormous desk and beaming a welcome. Laurie said he had all the answers he needed for the post now that I had applied but advised me that the Singapore Unit would be closing early next year. He said I'd do better to go to Nigeria where a long-term job was available with the Nigerian Air Force. I took his advice, took a short refresher instructional course at Plymouth and flew out to Kaduna, the northern capital of Nigeria, right on the edge of the Sahara desert.

141

At this stage in our family life, Sheila, 23, was a graduate of Bristol university, Chris, 20, was at St. Andrews University and very near to joining the Royal Air Force by the way of the University Air Squadron and Nonny was studying in the Queen Elizabeth College of London University. All three were doing very well and it was not long before Bunty joined me. Airwork Services for whom I worked for was searching for accommodation for all its employees at that time so we were housed in the Hamdala Hotel in Kaduna. Quite comfortable really, considering we had entered a country that was oven-hot throughout the year compared to the U.K. It seemed strange to have the weather cut and dried all the year round. In July, August and September frequent heavy rains, so heavy they needed 4ft. drains alongside the main roads to take away the water, severe thunder and lightning storms during which Nigerian electricians could be seen climbing up and down power poles to complete repairs; October to the New Year no rain, dusty with sandstorms straight off the Sahara. In Spring you could guarantee to book an outdoor party or barbeque on any given date five or six months ahead. Try that in Manchester. Once you became used to the high ambient temperature and wore clothes to suit, life was definitely enjoyable. Light rain occurred in Spring and was very welcome after five or six dry months and, for me, the only uncomfortable period was Autumn when it seemed impossible to avoid the effects of persistent perspiration.

It didn't take long before Bunty and I were comfortably housed in a large, cool, colonial-type house with an acre of paddock surrounding it, lemon, grapefruit and papaya trees. We found a very capable cook/steward and an indefatigable gardener who looked after us extremely well. At night we were 'protected' by Bedouins armed with swords who gathered together in groups for mutual protection. We shipped the car out to Lagos just before Bunty flew out and I was able to collect it without difficulty. What more could one want? Soon Bunty took up her favourite task of teaching, this time in an RC-run convent school in Kaduna, The Sacred Heart, teaching young children of many different nationalities.

At weekends we took advantage of the excellent weather and either drove into the countryside where Nigerians in their mud hut villages were fascinating to meet and talk to, or perhaps to areas where we knew wild life existed such as the rock hyrax – very like a guinea pig though its nearest relative is the African elephant. However, we drew the line at Baboon Rock, near Zaria, where whole families of baboons would gather and view our arrival with fear and distrust. They could have shortened our lives with ease. We also joined the local Field Society and went on outings on Sundays to the many interesting localities.

Our student pilots were mainly ex-University standard and there were no language difficulties. We trained them up to Wings standard based on the R.A.F. training system. However, I was intrigued by what happened to the new 'pilots' once they had left our tender care. They were moved to N.A.F. Kano, a large civilian/military airport, where they received operational training in the fighter pilot role from Russian instructors, in English, using Polish-built aircraft and then the Russian Mig operational ones. It seems that when flying took place there were English-speaking Russian interpreters available on the radio frequency in the Kano control tower in case of emergency or misunderstanding between instructor and student. In the mid-1970s a new scheme was introduced whereby our trainees were sent direct to the U.S.A. or to Russia for their jet training. Those who went to Russia were not greatly impressed by their treatment – all meals given were based on a diet of rice and chicken. However their principal fear was governed by the fact that their airfield was located three miles from the Chinese border and when the wind direction dictated an Easterly take-off a steepish turn at low climbing speed was needed to avoid an international incident.

The aircraft provided by the N.A.F. for us to train its students was the Italian Piaggio 409, a heavy and rather underpowered but quite manoeuvrable beast. Thank heavens the engine was reliable because this aircraft needed the application of full power when the wheels were selected 'down' prior to landing or it would lose height. The Nigerian engineering staff were quite efficient but were inclined to replace any items which became unserviceable rather than repair them. This, of course, meant that Piaggio spares became hard to come by and in the mid-1970s the N.A.F. was persuaded to dispense with the Piaggio fleet and buy the British Bulldog trainer. The first delivery of half-a-dozen of these new 'birds' was eagerly awaited at Kaduna and when the great day came the Nigerians were astonished to find that the formation leader (also the ferry company owner) was a trim young lady.

143

Airwork Services Ltd., supervised the maintaining and repairing of the new fleet and this made the aircraft last much longer. We had no problems at all with the Bulldog. It was much lighter than the Piaggio but handling techniques were mainly unchanged. For taxying, the nosewheel was steerable like most aircraft by putting pressure on the rudder pedals – very simple and easy for a new student to learn. One of my early students mystified me by leaning over to the left in the cockpit while taxying round a left-hand bend and to the right in a right-hand turn. This happened from the very beginning of his training. I asked him why he was doing this. He said, "I'm trying to help the aeroplane round the corner, Sah". I explained that it was not really necessary but, for a few flights he persisted. I thought about this peculiarity for some time and asked him, "When you were a boy did you ride a bicycle?" "Yes Sah, my uncle had a big bike and I could just reach the pedals and the handlebars. He supported me until I could go on my own." I said, "When you first went on your own and wanted to turn to the left, what did you do?" "I turned the handlebars to the left, Sah." "And what happened?" Pointing to his right he said, "I fell off over there, Sah". "So you learned that a two-wheeled vehicle needs help to turn a corner. However, I assure you a three-wheeler doesn't, though it was good of you to try."

I must be one of the few white persons alive who was awarded a Gold Medal in the African Olympics in the 1970s. The Closing Ceremony of the Games was held in Kaduna at the airport and the Nigerian Air Force was scheduled to carry out a formation fly-past as one of the final items. To ensure an accurate exercise an instructor occupied one seat in each aircraft although the 'Captain' of the aircraft was a Nigerian trainee. Each instructor involved was awarded a gold medal. I was reminded when the medal was given to me of a similar ceremony which took place during the war at the main airfield for Algiers, Maison Blanche. I had flown a Spitfire from Malta to Maison Blanche to have a major inspection carried out. An American photo-recce Squadron was based there flying Lockheed Lightning and an R.A.F. Squadron doing P.R with Spitfires, under Wing Commander Freddie Ball. I spent most of my three-day waiting time with these colleagues and on the second day a spruce-looking American official arrived and, from a small case he was carrying, he distributed an American D.F.C. (Distinguished

144

Flying Cross) to each of the U.S.A.F. pilots. When this part of the ceremony was completed he found that he had a few D.F.Cs. left over. These were then handed to pilots of the Spitfire Squadron. I don't think any records of those distributions were taken.

During the seven years Bunty and I had lived in Nigeria we had made good friends. One such, Tom Main, a College Principal, lives less than ten miles away from us now (another coincidence) and we entertain him regularly. Another, Alec Bryden, was the local agent for the Belgian airline, Sabena, during the time that they held the contract for government air passages to Europe. Alec had a fine African Grey parrot which seemed to know every trick in the trade. He was called Koko until she laid an egg and we had to rechristen her Coouette – with an appropriate liquid ceremony, of course.

When I joined the R.A.F. in 1941 along with a dozen or so other undergraduates from Reading University Air Squadron one of them was David Penn. Thirty five years later I was in a store in Kaduna searching for an acceptable bottle of wine from the wine-rack and I became aware of another man similarly engaged. We glanced at one another, as one does on these occasions, and while I was driving home I suddenly realised who it was. I phoned him immediately and the first thing he said was, "Keith Durbidge isn't it?" After the war he had returned to Reading to finish his degree in Agriculture and here he was, living in Kaduna and advising the Nigerian Government on their cereal crop plans. It's a very small world.

One day in Kaduna Bunty and I were astonished to receive a telegram from Sheila which said, "Married in Scotland. Sheriff, not shotgun". Shortly afterwards Nonnie wrote saying she had married an Australian and was planning to live in Australia! Both marriages have turned out very well and we have two granddaughters and two grandsons, all doing very well in the difficult modern world. I suppose I should have been delighted that, as a father of two brides, I had not been required to spend a sou but it did seem to be a bit of a hollow achievement. Chris was married after our return to the U.K. but that wedding took place at R.A.F. Cranwell with all the care, protocol and circumstances that the Services normally mustered.

Bunty and I left Nigeria in 1978 after seven years in the country. By this time the country had had a period of rule under a military government, mainly of Army officers. British administrators had been replaced by Nigerians as their tours of duty ended. Things rapidly began to fall apart. We were surprised by the way those well-tried systems of administration quickly failed their purpose and how soon bribery and corruption took over. It was time to go and let the Nigerians take over all aspects of government and control.

Once again I had been singled out by the gods for a piece of good fortune. Once again I read in a flying magazine 'something to my advantage'. This time there was an advertisement concerning a vacancy for the post of Chief Flying Instructor at a flying club in the north of Scotland, in fact at Dalcross, twenty minutes driving time from Bunty's home in Nairn. What a turn-up for the book! I overcame my immediate feeling of disappointment when I noticed the offer was nearly six months old and wrote at once in reply. It seems that no qualified flying instructor in Britain had any desire to take on this job in the frozen wastes of northern Scotland. No one had known, apparently, that the Moray Firth area of Scotland was one of the chosen zones of the R.A.F. for setting up flying training organisations because, no doubt, of its history of good flying weather and its uncluttered air space. Bunty and I were surprised and thoroughly delighted to get a reply offering me the post (I had not sent a photograph with my application) and asking me to start on the following Monday! Agreement was eventually reached with Airwork Services Ltd., the Nigerian Air Force and my fellow instructors that I should complete three months terminal service at Kaduna and then report to Dalcross to join the Highland Aero Club. In January 1978 I began the happiest period of my whole flying career.

# 24. Clear To Land, Tiddler

THE HIGHLAND AERO CLUB occupied the old R.A.F. wooden building which had housed the Post Office and the Battery Charging Room. The office was very small but cosy and became the focal point of all our activities. An old store room became the briefing room and the large battery room was rearranged into a crew room. A short walk to the hangar, just long enough to stress the vital points covered in the pre-flight briefing or to calm the nerves of anyone taking a trial flight. The situation was perfect for a flying club.

I spent many very happy years there before retiring when I failed my annual medical check because of what the specialist doctor said was an irregular heartbeat. I had no real cause for complaint having been flying or connected with aviation almost all of my adult life. Good fortune and happy coincidences had come my way and the gods had been kind throughout.

As a private Flying Club on a registered airport we were extremely fortunate. A full Air Traffic Control (ATC) staff, fully trained fire and accident section, a choice of six runway directions and limited bad weather facilities, as well as a large hangar to protect the aircraft and refuelling facilities at the end of the telephone. Add to this an emergency service available without cost from two nearby R.A.F. operational stations who were available 24 hours a day – who could ask for anything more?

Until the dying years of the 20th Century when Inverness was suddenly thrust upon the international scene for air transport we shared Dalcross with three airlines, Logan Air, British Airways and Dan Air, none of which had many aircraft movements. It was easy to learn when these few airliners were due to land or take off and the directions they would be operating in. There was no difficulty in fitting our movements in with theirs. Quite often, on seeing an airliner taxying out for take-off or one on a long final approach to land we could adjust our landing circuit procedures by telling ATC that we would complete a full orbit on our downwind or base leg to give the other aircraft the priority. ATC and the airline captains fully appreciated these arrangements and co-operated with us wherever possible. Those were the days when we could hold contests with other local flying clubs on a Saturday or Sunday afternoon and make full use of the airfield for long periods and be sure there'd be no interference. Spot landing and flour bombing competitions were very popular with all pilots and trainees especially when the bombing target, a white painted cross near the beginning of our N-S disused runway, was clearly disregarded by the bomb-dropper who aimed instead for the onlookers' cars parked nearby. A direct hit on somebody else's car with a pound of self-raising flour in a flimsy plastic bag was always greeted with roars of approval by all bar one.

In April 1981 I began to plan holding a spot landing competition in July. The American NASA space shuttle 'Columbia' had just made its successful landing at Cape Canaveral in the U.S.A. I decided to write to the two Columbia aeronauts as follows:

*The members of the Highland Aero Club wish to express their respect and admiration for your fine performance in bringing Columbia safely to earth. The touchdown was excellent. We would therefore like to offer you both free entry to our annual Spot Landing Competition which, this year, will be held in July. You can of course bring your own aircraft but would suggest that you do not choose Columbia. Our runway is only 1887 metres long, just adequate for our Cessna 152s. Congratulations to you both and many happy landings. Sincerely......."*

We were happy and slightly surprised to get this reply:

*Thank you very much for your congratulatory message. The spaceship Columbia is a truly remarkable vehicle and proved it on its very first mission! We enjoyed reading your good wishes and accept them on behalf of the thousands of NASA and contractor people whose combined energies made it possible for our new spaceship to perform so beautifully. This fantastic team made our Columbia's maiden voyage a dream come true. All of us are truly proud of this demonstrated capability of routine access to space. With appreciation for your sentimental and very best wishes, we remain sincerely yours, P.S. Appreciate the invitation to this year's Spot Landing Competition. Best regards to all who participate!*

I remember with pleasure a few people who passed our way during my twelve years close association with the Club.

There was Tommy MacDonald, the leading fireman, who was always kind and thoughtful, could turn his hand to any task, seemed to know everyone of note and was always nearby if help was needed.

Senga of the ATC staff – hated her name of Agnes (me too) so she turned it round. She helped our early soloists especially in circuit work and use of the radio and was always instrumental in getting passing RAF aircraft to do a low-level / high speed pass over the airfield. She loved a good 'beat up' and so did we.

Don Macgregor who came to the Club one day and asked, "I'm over seventy. Would I be able to get PPL (Private Pilot's Licence) do you think?" I told him, "Definitely. Provided you are not colour blind. You drive a car so your co-ordination must be satisfactory and you can start as soon as you like provided you satisfy the aeromedical doctor". He progressed steadily by flying at regular intervals and was as pleased as Punch when he passed all his tests and received his PPL. Unfortunately, a month or so after this success he failed his annual medical which meant that on his solo flights he had to take a qualified pilot with him. He didn't mind that too much and flew regularly until his death a year or two later. We carried out a fly-past at his funeral to the full satisfaction of his charming widow.

Giora Kahanov, an Israeli, became a British Airways captain having started his flying training with the Club.

Two young men in their late teens used to 'hang around' the Club doing odd jobs like cleaning aircraft, running errands etc., in return for free flights whenever a spare seat was available. One of them, we called him 'Snowball' on account of his very fair hair, was so keen on flying that he went on to become an airline pilot. Snowball absorbed instruction so well on his free flights that when one of our experienced Members offered him a spare-seat ride he accepted at once and did all the pre-flight checks for the pilot. When they returned an hour or so later the pilot said to me, "Who was that young man who flew with me? After take-off I climbed to a safe height and did a few exercises and then asked him if he would like to handle the controls to see what it feels like. He accepted immediately and the first thing he did was to trim the aircraft properly as I should have done" (Trimming is a facility available on most aircraft by which pilot fatigue is reduced).

My best student was a lady who, I felt sure, tried too hard in her spare time to be successful. She studied the text books and her own notes and often got so far ahead of the current requirement that we had to 'unlearn' some of the training sequences before we could make real progress. However, her determination to succeed overcame the problems which occasionally arose and progress to her PPL was rapid. The real secret towards becoming a pilot is to undertake training on a regular basis with short intervals in between flights, the shorter the better. 45-50 hours seemed to be the average time taken by a student who is able to get airborne regularly say, once a week. One trainee, I recall, took well over 60 hours because he could only attend now and then at long intervals when he was on leave from his job on an oil rig. This meant that to get his PPL would cost him about 40% more than normal. Anyway, with his job he could afford it.

I remember with gratitude how very supportive the instructional staff were. Big Tim Griffin did all the night flying for me – and some weekend work as well.

Ruth Wood, a very sound pilot, whose husband deserted her one day taking with him the car, the whole bank balance and all the available cash, leaving her to bring up their two teenage daughters. We persuaded her to take up instructional work and sent her on a flying instructor's Course. On her return she joined the staff and became a very successful and hard-working member. I went to her wedding to one of the Dalcross chopper pilots.

Colin Turnball, a quiet, gentle soul but a good instructor none the less. He had his own powered glider and spent his holidays gliding and skiing mainly in the Austrian Alps.

Liz Gliddon, married to a chopper pilot at Dalcross – What have chopper pilots got that lesser mortals don't possess? Liz was an excellent instructor who unfortunately left us for the warmer climes of Australia. She'll be back though.

One amusing memory I have from those happy days at Dalcross – I was just about to taxy out with a student when an Airline captain in a British Airways Viscount aircraft called up, "Dalcross, this is Speedbird 1877, request start up". The controller replied, "Clear start, temperature one three degrees". "Roger, Temp one three." When his two engines were running satisfactorily the pilot said, "Dalcross, Speedbird 1877, request taxy for er, er… where the hell are we going?" The ATC Controller said, "Well you are very likely the BA Flight to Stornoway at 1320 hours, going by my schedule". "Roger, thank you. Request taxy for Stornoway. Let's hope there's nobody on board for Orkney or Shetland."

What a confidence booster that would have been if the passengers could have heard the flying crew talking, especially the Captain.

Once, when Senga, the ATC Controller was on duty an RAF jet fighter flew past on its way home and Senga invited the pilot to do a fly-past. He said, "Wilco, do you have any other traffic?" "Negative, just a tiddler downwind on circuit work." "Roger, starting my run now." We watched as the jet did his run a few feet above the ground at about 600 mph. We continued our circuit and called on our final approach to the runway, "Dalcross, Tiddler on finals". Senga said, "Tiddler, clear to land or touch-and-go". I said, "Clear to land, Tiddler". It has always, to me anyway, been a welcome and very satisfying feature of aviation life that humour can find its place in a serious and sometimes dangerous activity.

# 25. Crazy, These Would-be Pilots!

THE HIGHLAND AERO CLUB'S annual 'holiday' taken in early May, was always spent on the small grass strip at Glenforsa on the beautiful Isle of Mull. There was an excellent hotel about 50 yards from the grass airstrip and the event attracted small aircraft from all over the country. An Irish contingent was a regular feature and was noted for its ability to drink copious quantities of beer with the locals and still be fit for the next day's activities. Getting to Mull from Inverness by road, carrying aviation fuel, the bicycle and other items too bulky for little aeroplanes was always a joy to me. The nearer we got to Mull the more the yellow poppies bloomed in the hedgerows. With every mile the weather seemed to improve and although transporting fuel on a ferry was illegal, our two 45-gallon drums of aviation spirit on the pick-up truck, was covered with tarpaulin. The bicycle and anything else we could use to hide them never attracted the attention of the ferry crew. (So we thought, but I'm sure a few blind eyes were turned.)

The hotel owners, an elderly couple, always welcomed us profusely because, as I like to think, not only did we occupy a number of their rooms but our members made sure that the temporary staff in the bar (employed at the beginning of the season and not always accustomed to bar services) made no mistakes. One year one of our younger members who was not accustomed to more than one beer joined the first night celebrations of yet another Mull weekend and drank a little more than he should have done. When the party was over and the celebrants went to bed he still had half a pint left. Early risers the next morning found him fast asleep on the floor of the corridor with his arm across the shoulder of the hotel's dog, a Great Dane, and the dog's head buried in the young man's chest. It seems he had been unable to find a way round the dog however much he tried and decided to get some sleep where he was. The dog, I'm sure, was delighted with all the attention he was getting.

Some members used the weekend at Mull to air their camping gear and could be seen erecting or dismantling their tents using the aircraft's wing as a shelter from any rain that might fall. They took their meals in the hotel and, of course, didn't need to take their pots and pans etc., with them. How convenient! Generally, the Mull weather was good throughout the time we were there.

Another grass strip we used at least twice a year was at Dornoch, a pleasant place to visit, right alongside the beach. We took special care to obey the rules governing the area because the RAF practice bombing range was only a mile away. Dornoch was not far away from Dalcross so we didn't need to stay overnight. Our usual spot landing and other competitions could be completed well within a day. This airstrip had a large shed which housed a past-its-normal-shelf-life fire engine and it was kept in running order by the local council. 'Running order' was rather a misnomer, really, more like 'walking order' because we took it out one day and, try as they might, our motor experts could not get more than eight mph out of her. (Why are ships, vehicles and machines given the personal pronoun 'her' instead of 'it', or for that matter even, 'him'?)

All of our daily servicing, maintenance, inspections and repairs were done by an excellent aircraft engineer/boffin/instrument basher, all contained in one slim, tall frame, that of John Horsfall. We teased him occasionally about his knowledge of light aircraft (he was also responsible for Dan-Air fleet and was expected to repair any light machine which landed at Dalcross and reported having problems). One Christmas we bought him a new hammer and chisel noting that his two current tools must surely be getting worn out with heavy usage on all these light flying machines. One year he had a very hard financial time – two Companies for whom he did a lot of maintenance work were extremely late in paying their bills, so late that he was in danger of having to abandon his tasks. Our Club could not have continued flying for very long if we lost his services but fortunately I was able to offer him cash relief to tide him over a difficult period. He looked after us very well throughout my fifteen years as Chief Instructor. Christmas is coming; I wonder if he needs a new chisel?

One of our students lived at Helmsdale, about half way to Wick and was employed on the railways. At his interview on joining the Club I asked him what his job was. He said he was a railway engineer. I thought this was a good start; any engineer would know about technical terms and wouldn't need to be taken laboriously into subjects like Boyle's law etc., during briefings. I mentioned this point to him and he disappointed me by saying that his pay packet described him as 'Railway Engineer' but actually he was a wheel-tapper and permanent way worker. Occasionally he was Station Master, Signals Chief and all general factotums at Helmsdale Station, being the only full-time railway employee there. Sometimes when he visited Inverness he would fly with us at Dalcross and when we took an aircraft to Wick to fly with students there he'd be one of them. He was quite a humourist and whenever I flew north to Wick or Kirkwall I was required to circle round above Helmsdale Railway Station and wait until he came out on to the platform and waved a green flag. I was then free to continue on my way. Crazy, these would-be pilots!

We had a visit one day from members of a German flying club in four light aircrafts who were touring Britain. One of them was a keen photographer and mad about castles. He was frequently to be seen, circling at low level over a choice example of the castle builder's art. He chose Balmoral Castle when the flag was flying not knowing that this meant the presence of the Queen. A complaint was made by someone in the royal party and the police took the matter up by phoning all likely flying clubs in the area. I was able to explain the activities of the Germans and their ignorance of the rules. This seemed to satisfy the police who said the matter was now closed and please brief the Germans accordingly. Some weeks later I received a very smart tie with a word of thanks for staving off any trouble that might have ensued. I thought of flying a flag over this Englishman's 'castle' but I realised it might be considered a trifle ostentatious; besides, I didn't have a flag to fly and if I had I was certainly not going to climb about the roof of my house (we had no chimneys) looking for somewhere suitable to secure it.

155

During his period of Service in the RAF, my son Christopher was looking after a dog for a colleague who had been posted to the Falklands. When his turn came to go there he asked us to look after Dylan, a glorious dark brown and white English Springer Spaniel. I really adored Dylan and so did Bunty. He had a wicked streak. When we first had him he lived outside in a kennel (on instructions from Chris) and, so our neighbours told us later on, every morning about six o'clock he would leave his kennel, leap the front garden hedge, spend an hour or more playing on the sea shore and, strictly on time, be back in his 'house' waiting for his breakfast as if he'd just woken up. Bunty and I knew nothing of this. We took him inside the first winter and he was so good in the house (cunning hound) that we disposed of the kennel. It seems a common ailment to all dogs of the Spaniel or Labrador breed that at about fourteen years their hind quarters become progressively weaker and they tend to drag themselves along. It was obvious to us that Dylan was in considerable discomfort or even pain when moving around and we felt we had to put him out of his misery. He was sixteen when we made the final decision. I had never seen Bunty cry as much before.

My flying career came to an end when, following an annual medical examination, I was told that my heartbeat was irregular and was therefore suspect and that my flying license would be suspended immediately. I suppose that the powers that be were right because I had a stroke some months later which put me in hospital. I don't miss the flying as much as I thought I would, possibly because I've had my share of getting airborne for half a century. I've had a really wonderful life with the love and support at every stage from Bunty for well over sixty years.

Retirement has not been difficult but I seem to be busier and the days go by more quickly. I've had time to remember how very fortunate Bunty and I have been as parents and grandparents. All our children are either handsome or beautiful and all have been educationally brilliant. We were able to see our Australian grandsons, Mark and Andrew, during visits when they were growing up and we've been particularly lucky to watch Davina and Esme throughout their childhood, teens and now in their late twenties. They are both particularly good-looking and full of life, thoughtful for others and keen to help in any activity.

## Crazy, These Would-be Pilots

Right now I'm wondering if I can find the time to write my memoirs as requested by my big daughter, Sheila. I suppose I'd better start 'cause she is bigger than I am. I trust half a dozen pages will be enough.

Let me see, now, where shall I start? How about my schooldays and Caversham? The opening sentence should be arresting or humorous, even argumentative or instructional. I'll go for the last one, having been an instructor for many years and bring old Horatio into play....

# Epilogue

Born: 1 June 1921 in Caversham, Reading
Died: 2 May 2011 in Nairn, aged 89

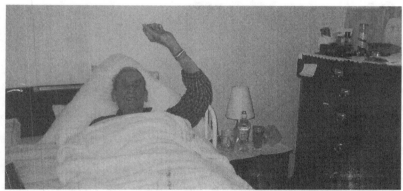

This photograph was taken some years after Keith's stroke. He had just written an inspirational message as Life Vice President to the ACA members in March 2011.

"Too many clubs and organisations are having to disband due to ageing members or changes in circumstances and alas, ours is one of them. It is my unhappy duty as Vice President to bother you with an official declaration that our Branch is disbanding. We have had many good times over the years, and achieved much, which I sincerely hope you will enter in gold lettering in your diary - if you keep one. If you don't have a diary, then put our achievements and any pearls of wisdom in bold lettering on the ceiling above your bed. By this method, they will fill your waking thoughts, and possibly inhabit your dreams.
I don't often issue Pearls of Wisdom, as they are very expensive and should be looked after with great care (that is why they should be written on the ceiling above your bed). This is the point of my peroration when I would normally intersperse a truism, but instead I will share an old joke:
Q. Why do we say AMEN instead of AWOMEN?
A. Because we sing hymns and not hers

You see, the old ones *are* the best ones.

I have not been able to attend our meetings on a regular basis over the past few years, but I would like to take this opportunity to wish you all well and to hope that success rewards your endeavours."

159

# Keith Durbidge

## Pilot who overcame air sickness to become a war reconnaissance photographer

■ **Keith Durbidge DFC DFM, airman. Born: 1 June 1921 in Caversham, Reading. Died:2 May, 2011 in Nairn, aged 89.**

AS A novice airman, Keith Durbidge had a less than auspicious start to his flying career. When every training flight made him physically sick, he feared he might not have what it would take to make it as an RAF pilot. All the more remarkable then that he went on not only to be decorated for his courage, unarmed in the skies, in face of the enemy but also to produce some of the finest reconnaissance photographs of the Second World War and to inspire generations of pilots with his infectious enthusiasm for flying. His was the spirit that epitomised the determination and derring-do of Britain's young wartime airmen.

Born in Berkshire, as a boy he was fascinated by speeding transport, running from school every afternoon to stand on the railway bridge in time to catch the Cheltenham Flyer hurtle below him at 80mph at 3.23pm.

When his father took a job on the railways in Nigeria in 1930, he went to Reading Blue Coat School as a day boy, becoming a boarder there the following year when his mother followed her

husband to Africa.

And at the age of 15 he was taken on by the headmaster as a pupil-teacher. In return, he received full board and lodging and £2 pocket money each month. When war broke out, while he was studying to go to university, his duties were extended to include fire-watching and air raid precautions.

He was 19 when he went to Reading University in 1940 to study science. He joined the Air Training Squadron in 1941 and at the end of his first university year he applied to join the RAF for aircrew training.

After a train journey to Gourock and a trip across the Atlantic on a liner to Halifax, his flight training began at the Canadian Air Force Station at Moncton, New Brunswick and later Ponca City in Oklahoma.

With his first flight, on 3 November, 1941, began the despair of suffering air sickness. Not one to give in easily however, he managed to overcome the nausea and, taking off on Stearmans, BT 13s (Vultee Valient) and AT6 Harvards, he finally accumulated his 187 hours dual, solo and night flying, earned his wings and was promoted to sergeant.

Returning to Britain, he started his photographic reconnaissance career more by accident than design. All the young air-

men wanted to get into the Spitfire squadrons but, while they were queuing up, Durbidge was otherwise engaged chatting to a young woman in a bar.

When he finally joined the end of the queue the last two places left were for PR – because no-one had had a clue what it stood for. It turned out to be photographic reconnaissance and, happily for him, it was a skill that required a Spitfire.

He started his career at RAF Fraserburgh on a Supermarine Spitfire and flew a sky blue version of the plane, camouflaged to dodge the German aircraft. Nicknamed the flying petrol bowser, the PR Spitfires carried no guns but were fitted with internal and external fuel tanks, allowing them to power away from danger. They also had a range of 1,750 miles but with no pilot relief tube and sorties often lasting five hours, the fliers had to develop extreme bladder control.

He left for Malta in 1942, joining 69 Squadron commanded by Wing Commander Adrian

160

"Warby" Warburton. His key tasks were to monitor and photograph all the enemy's land, sea and air forces, especially in North Africa and to get coverage of the three main Italian naval bases at Taranto, Naples and Messina, whenever an allied convoy was due to set off from Gibraltar or Alexandria.

Durbridge was involved in pre-invasion reconnaissance of the landing beaches in Sicily in 1943 and that February was awarded the Distinguished Flying Medal. Due to the heavy workload, the squadron was split into two with the high-level reconnaissance Spitfires becoming 683 Squadron. Soon after that move he was commissioned as a pilot officer.

By this time he had: survived a couple of attempts at sabotage; been strafed overnight in the desert while his plane was awaiting repair; spotted more than 100 Junkers Ju52/3m German transport planes on an airfield at Naples and realised that the Germans were trying to supply Rommel by air as sea efforts had failed. Subsequently, almost all the transport planes were destroyed by fighters from Malta.

On one occasion, having had to land in Bone in Algeria because there was something wrong with his plane, and surviving with his colleagues in Malta on very meagre rations, he went out and bought as many oranges as he could cram into his Spitfire for the return journey.

With the war in North Africa over, he was posted back to the UK as a PR flying instructor at Lulsgate Bottom in Somerset and then to Dyce, to train pilots, before going to RAF Benson, flying over Norway and France and looking for V1 and V2 sites.

He joined 542 Spitfire PR Squadron in 1944 flying Mk X and Mk XI Spitfires, and later the powerful Griffon-engined Mk 19.

When he was sent to assess bomb damage in the Ruhr following an RAF raid, he had just taken his photographs and turned for home when he saw a vast armada of planes coming towards him. The 50 US Fortresses, escorted by Mustangs, didn't recognise him as an ally and he was attacked. Thanks to the Griffon engine he was able to climb quickly away to safety.

On another occasion, he avoided being blown up by a Messerschmidt rocket by just 15 seconds by flying into cloud and circling on instruments until he estimated the enemy would have run out of fuel.

At the end of the war, he was sent to Berlin to fly information and documents back to Churchill and entered Hitler's bunker, bringing home two of his crystal glasses.

His immense skills were recognised in March 1945 when he received the Distinguished Flying Cross from King George VI. The following month he married his wife Bunty and after the war he became an instructor for the Nigerian Air Force and later the Highland Aero Club in Inverness, where his students included Pink Floyd's lead singer, Dave Gilmour.

A Highland Aero Club trophy for aerobatic skills and other flying skills is named and awarded annually in Durbidge's honour.

Relaxed, modest, amusing and charming to a fault, he was greatly admired for his exploits in the sky both in wartime and in civilian life. He was widowed last year and is survived by his children Sheila, Chris and Nonny and four grandchildren.
**ALISON SHAW**

### Obituaries and appreciations

The Scotsman welcomes obituaries and appreciations from contributors as well as suggestions of possible obituary subjects.
Please contact Ashley Davies, Gazette Editor,
The Scotsman,
108 Holyrood Road,
Edinburgh EH8 8AS
(0131-620 8610 after 1pm).
adavies@scotsman.com

# Index

# Index